The Well-Tempered Tongue

The Politics of Standard English
in the High School

The Well-Tempered Tongue

The Politics of Standard English in the High School

John Willinsky

Foreword by Edgar Friedenberg

 Teachers College, Columbia University
New York and London

Published by Teachers College Press, 1234 Amsterdam Avenue,
New York, NY 10027

A hardcover edition of this book is published by Peter Lang Publishing, Inc., New
York, NY. It is reprinted here in paperback by arrangement with the publisher.

Library of Congress Cataloging-in-Publication Data

Willinsky, John, 1950–
   The well-tempered tongue : the politics of standard English in the high school /
John Willinsky ; foreword by Edgar Friedenberg.
     p. cm.
  Reprint. Originally published: New York : P. Lang,
  c1984. (American university studies. Series XIV, Education ; vol. 4)
     Bibliography: p.
     Includes index.
     ISBN 0-8077-2925-6 (pbk.)
     1. English language—Study and teaching (Secondary)—Nova Scotia—
Case studies. 2. Language and education—Social aspects—Nova
Scotia—Case studies. 3. Students—Nova Scotia—Language (New
words, slang, etc.)—Case studies. I. Title.
[LB1631.W44 1988]
428′.007′12716—dc19
                                       88-20073
                                        CIP

Manufactured in the United States of America
93 92 91 90 89 88   1 2 3 4 5 6

To Pam

Contents

Foreword

"I realize," John Willinsky observes of language in the introduction to **The Well-Tempered Tongue**, "that I am making it over into a political struggle; language may seem to be cast solely as a rhetorical and ideological practice entailing negotiation, resistance and complicity. This is hardly all that language is, though. Rather, it is what happens to language in the school's effort to create both students and teachers of English. Language becomes so instrumental in these efforts that those other, fondly imagined, capabilities—of the sort that might first start English teachers on their careers—tend to get lost. But not completely, or in every instance."

Yet, language surely **is** a political struggle: an ideological practice entailing negotiation, resistance and complicity, as most Canadians are by now presumably aware. One of the most striking aspects of this study is that nobody else in this country saw the necessity of doing it earlier. It is perhaps equally remarkable that it was ever done at all. For the functions of language considered here are precisely those that the people who share it are least likely to be aware of, and are usually reluctant to analyze; the language itself, indeed, tends to conspire against those who would identify its modes of operation. This would be true no matter what institution the sociolinguist chose to observe; but it is especially true in the school, which is the official custodian of language usage and the administrative agency charged with the maintenance of cultural hegemony. Tactful and moderate as Dr. Willinsky's account is, it still threatens to blow the schools' cover. How could it not?

In a sense, **The Well-Tempered Tongue** is a disheartening work. It so clearly establishes "that the school has contributed, by intention and omission, to the greater articulation of some and the silencing of other"—and not, usually, in either case, the ones I would personally have preferred if this unhappy but hardly unanticipated result cannot be avoided. It probably cannot; for Willinsky makes it clear that what the school does to students with language is central to its social function: its way of defining them to themselves, of channeling and limiting their aspirations as well as their power to recognize what is happening to them and to influence the process decisively on their own terms. Many recognize of course that what the school tells them about themselves ain't necessarily so; but the audience that greets this observation with indulgent laughter wouldn't be caught dead anywhere near Catfish Row itself.

There is, then, not much probability that a book like this will lead to major changes in the way schools actually function; if it did, the schools would lose their present political support and their modicum of second-hand political power. Changes—even major changes—in the process of schooling do occur as consequences and sometimes as aspects of shifts in the balance of political power; but schooling is not a major cause of such shifts. Willinsky understands this far better than most students and critics of the process of schooling; and he clearly neither expects nor intends that his book will occasion widespread reform in the practice of teaching English or any other official language. His purpose is the more modest one that students "will be armed or at least protected against the full appropriation. . .of clarity and respectability, or in Foucault's terms, of knowlege and power. . .As we have a tongue which would be taught to be well-tempered, we shouldn't flinch from teaching it more honestly, if not more joyously and freely."

These are the book's concluding words; and, indeed, it does lead to the conclusion that joy and freedom in the classroom would be distinctly incongruous. What leaves me more hopeful that students may come to respect themselves more fully through their own idiosyncratic use of language is not any prospect that the schools will acquiesce in it; but that the school's role in hegemony is increasingly contested and not to be taken for granted. It is genuinely witty of Boy George to have named his group **Culture Club**; and many young people whom the schools perceive as articulate have expressed their eagerness to join the club on the terms offered. Viewed in the proper light there is, after all, something appealing about the concept of culture.

Some of the hidden and not-so-hidden injuries of class that the school inflicts by its use of language may be redressed or even forestalled by current alterations in the hegemonic order. This isn't just a matter of learning languages, heavily discounted in advance by adults, from the peer group or rock video—though I would not disparage the liberating and esteem-enhancing functions of these. But a higher proportion of young people than of their elders now read some languages that their elders cannot so easily disparage—or master. I have been struck by the irony of the fact that computer languages, though sometimes celebrated as the key to the discourse of the future—an improbable prediction—are never celebrated for their clarity and precision, their syntactical rigour; though Latin coasted downhill for a couple of centuries on its more dubious claims to promote these as mental qualities. Students have probably always known, especially if they were socially or ethnically stigmatized, that they stood a better chance of surviving their education if they became adept at clearing their memories of the school's commands and leaving a few bytes for their own subroutines in defiance of its efforts to peek and poke, especially when their output was in the graphic mode. This has always been basic, but now there is an official language for deciding what to do about it. IF school is greater than or equal to life, THEN GO TO school. IF it is less than life, THEN BREAK. RUN. More sophisticated responses may of course be programmed, and often are.

It will probably always be true, as Willinsky argues, that people who are fluent in a higher status language will get more satisfaction. But it is no longer as true as it used to be that what the school says, goes. How it says it still retains a measure of authority, and the power to make young people who use language differently doubt whether they have anything to say at all. But today, in the Age of Jackson, they may not doubt it so much. I'm old enough to remember when we thought Sunrise semester was great television—though, personally, I preferred the Flintstones, live—but I don't think the Canadian Radio-Television and Telecommunications Commission is entertaining an application for a 24-hour pay channel of high school or even university classes. At least in the short run, then, and in some aspects of life, there can be real progress. Enjoy, enjoy.

Edgar Friedenberg
Dalhousie University

Preface

This is a study of language in a Canadian high school. It is concerned with the work of the school's English department—both in what it intends and in what it accomplishes. It is equally concerned with the sense which the students have made of standard English. Student competencies in standard English have not been measured in this study; it considers the consequences of measurements and judgements already made. It looks for the significance of standard English in the teachers' interpretation of the measures, and in the students' responses to the judgements. To grasp this significance, one must understand the importance which language differences have assumed in this society, as well as the part they play in the school's English program.

Standard English, as we shall discover, is a convenient abstraction, variously conceived as part of the cultural heritage of the English speaking world, as the discourse of logic and precision, and as currently necessary for effective communication among educated people. For the students with whom I spoke, it proved a much simpler thing: the standard was the dialect you affected to get through a job interview without "sounding dumb." At any rate, the range of concerns and claims for standard English is enough to justify this attempt to specify, as exactly as possible, what it can mean to the participants of four English classes in a senior high school.

Standard English is a term which has only recently found its way into the schools. In simpler times, there had only been English. Teachers spoke it for the most part; they wrote textbooks in it and about it; and they tried their best to teach it to their students. Questions of language style were simply issues of correctness. Mistakes were, in essence, a misuse of the language. However, this abyss of wrongness, in which so many of the students spent their days chatting amicably, has in the last decade been transformed into a less dismal state. In English curriculum documents, misuse has become a matter of "nonstandard usage" and "ineffective communication." The implications of slothfulness have been set aside, as the schools have grown more sensitive and linguistically wise.

The educational status of language differences, then, is hardly a new topic, A decade and more ago, it was more thoroughly in vogue. At that time, William Labov and Basil Bernstein were each in their way slaying the myth of linguistic deprivation, though not without taking the odd swipe at each other. Linguistic prejudice and cultural imperialism were exposed and about to be dispelled. Over the last ten years, this concern for the misrepresentation of language differences has filtered down into the classroom, suffusing along the way educational journals, conference presentations and workshops, curriculum guidelines and experimental programs. Having gone that far, it had, in the way of educational practices, gone far enough. The recent retrenchment in the economic climate has been matched by a swing back among educational interests, first to the basics in such areas as standards in language and the school and then onto excellence in their mastery.

If the issue of language differences has seemed to have exhausted itself among educators, if it has run its course, then it would appear to be the right moment to measure the impact which the issue has had on the schools. A decade ago language became the central issue in the equality of educational opportunity, and it is time to assess the consequences of that concern on the teachers and students of English; it is time to talk with the students who began school in the early 1970's and discover the sense they are now making of language and of themselves as language users.

I sought out this understanding of language in a Nova Scotian high school, which provides a rather interesting meeting ground of educational themes from both Britain and the United States. For example, the head of the school's English department spoke of Bernstein's work in England on linguistic codes, while the teacher in charge of the Writing Centre found the American work done on black dialects handy in describing the language habits of his black students; the teachers were experimenting with a British Language for Learning approach, and they were trying to reach the less avid students with the American gang novels of S. E. Hinton. But then Margaret Atwood, Farley Mowat and other Canadian writers were being used as well, and ultimately a Canadian amalgan of influences was at work among concerns which confront English teachers everywhere.

One concern in the teaching of English is that while teachers may confidently measure a student's grasp of a text, they cannot so easily gauge the notions of language and literature which the students take away with them. All that is readily apparent is that a lesser degree of enthusiasm prevails among the students than in the English teacher; the difference in caring seems to be about language and the wonders to be worked in words. But as I discovered over the course of the study, the students cared very much about language, making a number of fine and sometimes literary distinctions about its use and importance. That this interest in language goes wanting in the English class is an underlying concern of this book, and one with which I believe English teachers would appreciate some help.

The English teacher's enthusiasm and training have been for language in literature. Yet the language issue they actually face, the question of a student's regard for literacy and standard English, is not a literary one. Often coming between teacher and student is a conflict in language, a conflict over the more fundamental lessons on what counts in language. The conflict can undermine the willing suspension of disbelief and the pursuit of literary texts. This book delves into the undercurrent of language interests in the English class as it documents the range and instances of language attitudes and knowledge among the teachers and students. The postures of resistance and indifference, compliance and enthusiasm which the English teacher faces can be understood as varying expressions of the students' grasp of the issues in language.

Before describing the teaching and learning of English in the school I visited, I present in the first two chapters of the book an introduction to standard English as a social entity. In the first chapter, I examine both the status of standard English as an agreed-upon body of exemplary English and the virtues—moral and intellectual—which have underwritten its claim as the prestige form. Such virtues have been the force driving English teaching for some time. But beyond motivating teachers, the qualities of the standard have become deeply entangled in the debate over social inequality which troubles, time and again, the conscience of the democratic state. The explanations for inequality began to arise out of Binet's work with IQ and the testing movement in the early part of this century. By the 1960's, the attempt to explain the differences in achievement—a moral and psychological quest, in essence—had arrived at a theory of linguistic deprivation (for example, Bereiter and Englemann 1966), which was assessed, of course, against the standard. If only all students had a proper language.

In the second chapter, I consider the context which the schools and the teachers provide for the students' education in language. A number of studies have pointed out that in the curriculum and in the teachers' expectations and social mores, the students have had to contend with such seemingly extraneous matters as gender, race and social disadvantage. These issues affect the development of language and literacy among the students, and, as I mentioned, a number of them have received remedial attention in the schools over the course of the last decade.

The English curriculum guidelines of the Nova Scotia Department of Education, for example, have responded over these years to the language question in a blending of educational and political interests.

The senior high school in Nova Scotia where I conducted the study during the school year of 1981-2 is the focus of chapters three to six. The school had approximately 1,200 students and was located close enough to the centre of the community to draw students from both ends of town. The study consisted of observing four English classes selected from the extremes of the program both in grade and course level—at the grade ten level, a general level (10G) and an advanced academic level (10A); at the grade twelve level, a general level (12G) and an enriched academic level (12A). I interviewed the four English teachers at the beginning of the term and kept up my discussions with them as the study progressed. Each of the students in the four classes wrote a forty-item Sentence Completion Test on standard English, literacy and English classes (with an extra 10G class included to bolster the meager size of that group). Of the ninety-six students who wrote the test, I interviewed twenty of them for a more detailed response to language and standard English.

The English department's program in language and literature is described in chapter three. There the importance of standard English is found in diverse places: bound within the covers of the department's traditional English Primer; unfolding in the new Language for Learning movement; expressed in the talk about literature in class; marked on the page in the evaluation of the students' work. The streaming of courses and students is the principal structural feature of the program; the divisions are rooted in a basic apprehension of differences in the students' facility with standard English and their commitment to its interests. However, teaching language in the streams encourages a moral distinction between the futures which the students are imagined to inherit in the language.

After discussing what has been taught, I turn in chapter four to what has been learned. A statistical analysis of the individual items from the Sentence Completion Test revealed a number of significant differences between the language attitudes of the general level and the advanced level students, as well as between the sexes. Different senses of the standard and the consequences of propriety emerged from among the students, while agreement prevailed on the important moments in language and on the thrust of the English classes. The standard proves throughout the analysis to have a certain hold on the minds, if not the tongues, of the students. Yet surprisingly, the students' ideas of the standard often have as little to do with communication as they do with literature.

The statistical depiction of students attitudes takes on human face in chapter five where the range of students responses is presented through interviews with eight of the students. The students' views move from a superficial to a profound regard for standard English. Apart from this spectrum, two of the eight students took another tack, going beyond and somewhat against the school in their interest in literacy. A number of the students in their comments also moved the question of language differences out of the school and into the neighborhoods of their differing fortunes. They were not content to treat language as an academic issue; for each of them it is another aspect of finding themselves in the school and beyond.

In the final chapter, with the better part of the issue in hand, a number of alternatives are considered for the English program in the school including recent language texts and literacy theorists. A most promising starting point to improve this education in language, I suggest, is to begin with the prevalent language attitudes of the students and staff. To challenge and explode the misconceptions, so often belitting and based on exaggerated notions of language differences, may well offer the student a different future in the language. In disentangling some of the aesthetic, political and pedagogical issues entailed in the English program, the teacher may be able to offer literacy as a more accessible social resource, open to more students who might then become intent on using their education to say something more.

There is one final issue I wish to raise in this preface. I have described how I intend to treat standard English as a social fact, as a matter of interpretation and consequence. I realize that in this approach I am making language over into a political struggle; it becomes caught up in an ideological infrastructure. Words become both the weapons and the targets for people securing their position in the linguistic community.

But, of course, this is hardly all that language is. Rather, my interest is in the fact that this can happen to language through the school's efforts to create both students and teachers of English. Language distinctions, such as those between standard and nonstandard, become so instrumental in the business of schooling, that those other, fondly imagined capabilities of language tend to get lost. Thus in this study I have set aside the power of language found in the words of a friend or in a line from a book or a song. This is the language which first brought many of us into the teaching of English. It is lost often enough in English classes to stop and ask why. But setting it aside should not be taken as a denial that many in the school still find this other more encouraging power in language. The possibility—through friends, music and books—of escaping the politics of differences and judgements may be attributable to the school as well, but often as only an epiphenomenon. The school does house friends, a number of approachable adults, and quite a few books—there is often nothing quite like it in the community. However, these less political and very personal capabilities of people talking and reading, singing and writing, are not, as I intend to demonstrate, the only ways in which language is worked in the schools.

Acknowledgements

The study presented in this book was originally supported by the Win Davies Memorial Scholarship granted by the Ontario Public School Teachers' Federation. The Federation is to be commended for permitting teachers in this way to look thoughtfully and critically at their own work. In this instance that looking took the form of a doctoral dissertation which was guided and advised by the relentless intelligences of Edgar Friedenberg and Toni Laidlaw. They repeatedly alerted me to what might have been overlooked. Without relinquishing any of the responsibility for this work, I acknowledge the extent to which they have opened my eyes. I also want to express my debt to the students and teachers of "Kipling High School" who participated in the study; their candor and interest have made this work possible, while their friendliness made working with them a pleasure. Still it should not be surprising, given the nature of my findings, that a few of the teachers were later to object to my description of the situation at the school. While I stand by its accuracy and acuity, I do believe that the pattern is common to the institution, rather than unique to "Kipling High School," and applies in many instances to my own work in this trade and to that of other, much finer teachers of English.

The Canadian College of Teachers through the Wilfred R. Wees Doctoral Thesis Award has contributed to the study's transformation into a book. Shari Avery has expertly set the work into type under the patient supervision of Bob Wright; my gratitude goes out to both of them for the time and skill they have committed to this project. I have also been well served by the advice provided my editor at Peter Lang Publishing, Jay Wilson. Much closer to my home, my wife, Pam, has worked hard with me on the final editing of the text; though, in truth, this is only a small part of the reason I have dedicated this book to her.

I wish to thank Clark Blaise and the **Canadian Forum** for permission to reprint a passage from the short story "South" (1982) and Delacourte Press for permission to cite from Richard Brautigan's **The Tokyo-Montana Express** (1980). Portions of this work have appeared in **The English Quarterly** and **The McGill Journal of Education**.

John Willinsky
Sault Ste. Marie

1
The Contemporary Setting
Of Standard English

What one needs to understand is how...**the tools of freedom become the sources of indignity.**

Richard Sennett and Jonathan Cobb

Standard English has a fine linguistic pedigree which can be traced back through such designations as Received Pronunciation and the King's English to an East Midland form of Middle English, more recently of London.[1] But to briefly consider the historical development of the standard, until the eighteenth century there was little interest in constructing for the language a prescriptive grammar of the sort which had ruled Latin since classical times and which governs the standard today. Philip Sidney could boast toward the end of the sixteenth century in his **An Apology for Poetry** that English "hath that praise that it wanteth not grammar: for grammar it might have but it needs it not" (Sidney 1970, p. 85). The printing press, the Reformation and the rising middle class had given vernacular English its first real currency as a language of consequence and capability. The Elizabethans had created eloquence out of English, and the Puritans, in more sombre tones, found it indispensible for widespread edification.

But a sense of linguistic and national inadequacy in the seventeenth century prompted a number of concerned voices to be raised in favour of improving and purifying the English tongue (Jones 1953). In response a great number of grammatical rules and prescriptions were put forward to refine the vernacular and guide the unsure speaker; the linguistic feat of the eighteenth century was to instill the mother tongue as a matter of correctness in usage (Leonard 1962). The new grammarians drew their precedents from the example of the classical languages, from a desire for consistency and analogy in the language, and from national interests. Alas, a standard was fixed at that point, though not for good by any means nor without dissension on what was literate usage. Nonetheless, a prescribed grammar had taken hold of English, one which allowed the educated speaker "to judge every phrase and form of construction, whether it be right or not," in the words of Robert Lowth, a best-selling grammarian of the period (cited by Myer 1966, p. 225). This doctrine of correctness in English usage would seen to serve an anxious genteel class underwriting its claim to refinement and propriety, its right to succeed a faltering aristocracy.

All of Europe had been affected by the decline of Latin and the increasing importance of the vernacular languages. Many countries turned to language academies in the sixteenth and seventeenth centuries to ensure the worthiness of their language as an instrument of refinement and learning. But in England and America, the language academy was to be successfully resisted, though it had been advocated by such notables as Defoe and Swift in England, and John Quincy Adams in America (Baron 1982). Free of a single authority in establishing a standard, the prestige form of English was to remain to some degree less fixed and rigid than the governed forms of, for example, French or Swedish (Seppanen 1981).

Yet without benefit of an academy, there was still a strong sense of difference and distinction to be had from the way people spoke English. During the nineteenth century, the schools became a major means of maintaining the distinctions between standard and nonstandard, and informing the public of the moral and logical superiority of a well-tempered tongue. In American schools of the nineteenth century, for example, grammar was upheld as "an employment calculated to exclude those frivolous pursuits, and that love of ease and sensual pleasure which enfeables the mind," as L. Murray described it in 1795 (cited by Baron 1982, p. 149). The twentieth century high school students, with whom I spoke in this study, still sensed some part of this moral distinction. Though they hadn't the advantage of being admonished outright by the likes of Mr. Murray, they had been instructed for a good number of years on the correct nature of their mother tongue. The prestige form of English became finally in its claim no more, but no less, than the standard (which is rarely capitalized, designating a benchmark in the language rather than a dialect).

In the current language curriculum guides provided by the provincial Department of Education to the teachers of Nova Scotia, standard English needs no introduction. In fact, it barely requires mention. It is, though, not forgotten, but constantly alluded to in terms of the "effective," "good (appropriate)," "required" and "conventional" (Nova Scotia Department of Education: NSDE 1978, pp.1-3). If there is a definition of it at all, it is through a statement of what standard English is not:

> 'he don't,' 'that's some nice' or 'she done good'...are not considered by most people to be appropriate in many of the speaking and writing situations which will arise for children. (NSDE 1978, p. 2)

Or more bluntly: "our educated society tends to consider 'them books' as being the speech of the ignorant" (NSDE 1972, p. 6). But ultimately, it would appear that no explicit definition is required because "the teacher of English in...Nova Scotia knows full well that it is his job to do something about such speech" (ibid.). Actually the guideline writers did well to avoid pinning it down any more precisely; it does not serve to start defining the unspoken understandings central to one's work.

But as an outsider to this understanding, I would like to begin with the explicit claims which have been made for this form of language. Andrew Wilkinson, those writings are cited in several of the provincial English guidelines, provides what must be very close to a common sense definition of standard English: it is "a form of English acceptable to the international community of educated speakers of the language" (1972, p. 224). As it turns out, the question of acceptability to an educated community had been empirically tested. This research gives some suggestion of how definite and fixed a body of knowledge this language form constitutes.

Some years ago Sterling Leonard (1932) submitted 230 expressions 'of whose standing there might be some question' to 229 concerned professionals—linquists, English teachers, authors, businessmen. They were asked to classify the expressions as either literary English, colloquial English, or popular (illiterate). There was only unanimous agreement on four of the expressions—all of them having been placed in the third category. Myers, in his review of the study, provides some of the more curious disputes: "I **drove** the car around the block" received condemnation from six per cent of the judges as being illiterate, and only fifteen percent would approve of it as literary (1966, p. 286). "**Under these circumstances**" fared even worse, while "**Who** are you looking for?" was condemned by only twenty-five percent of the judges (ibid.). The public response to the study was also a point of some interest:

> [T]here were outraged protests—in the school rooms, on editorial pages even from the pulpit .... [I]t was feared that after our language had become tasteless

and meaningless gibberish, the loss of respect for law and decency in all areas would soon follow. (Myers 1966, p. 287)

The public clearly considered standard English to be a matter of morality and public order. What was actually threatened by the study was a doctrine of correctness that can be called upon with some confidence. I imagine that it was difficult to accept that a standard had never really existed in the infallible and eminently logical manner which would have justified its superiority. The excited voices cited above declared this indeterminacy to be a sign of "liberal" teachers "letting down the bars" (ibid.). The spirit and substance of such an attack is, of course, alive and well today. John Simon (1980) is currently giving it a particularly articulate voice.

A few years after Leonard's work, Albert Marckwardt and Fred Walcott brought the same expressions for judgement before the higher authority of the **Oxford English Dictionary** and **Webster's New International.** Their subsequent publication,**Facts about Current English Usage** (1938), further weakened the edifice of a single coherent standard language. One third of the expressions which had been generally classified as "illiterate" in the Leonard study proved to have a place in the realm of standard English (Myers 1966, pp. 287-8). Myers suggests that as a result of these two studies "the simple division between good and bad English gradually lost ground to the idea that there could be various kinds of satisfactory English" (p. 288). It is, of course, one objective of this study to ascertain how much ground has been lost and to what sort of new terrain we have moved. At any rate, Wilkinson's definition of standard English would seem to suggest a too coherent and fixed body of language practices, even for a dialect very much absorbed in its own consistency and adherence to rules.

There have been other attempts to describe what is intended by the term "standard English." The noted linguist, Leopold Bloomfield (1927) formally introduced the distinction between "literate" and "illiterate" speech, laying the groundwork for Bernstein's codes in more ways than one. Bloomfield notes that literary language functions as a guide to standard speech, so that we "are able to agree what is and what is not 'good'—that is standard" (pp. 435-6). There is a very fine line in this—marked by the use of inverted commas—between description and prescription. He does point out that "bad" and "incorrect" forms are not the result of carelessness or ignorance, as the "layman" might suppose (p. 432). But ultimately he affirms that "there is such a thing as correct English," and it is to be found in adhering to the rules of the written word (ibid.).

What he fails to point out is that this notion of the printed text as an authority can be attributed to the invention of moveable type; prior to Gutenberg, manuscript culture "had no power to fix the language," as McLuhan has noted (1962, p. 229). The written word "had continued to evolve after the pattern of the spoken language" in both the Latin and the vernacular languages until the sixteenth century (ibid.). The printed text—standardized in authoritative editions—became the model for language use. Protestantism played a part in this, as it marked a return to the authority of the Book, and people were asked to adhere to the letter of the law.

Bloomfield's description of the standard as the literate was hardly very helpful or much of a discovery. Those who worked so hard at advancing a doctrine of correctness fully intended it to govern the entire range of language uses. Those who were attracted to the authority of print would naturally try to draw on this authority in their speech. Bloomfield's analysis did not just serve to act as a reminder of this linguistic fact. It also had the effect of placing "written English" at the centre, with all other non-standard dialects being assessed as deviations away from this standard.[2] As a natural history of language forms it is rather absurd. The most obvious distinction has been missed; standard English has been made out of the vernacular and into a prestige dialect by conscious design.

Anthony Kroch's (1978) research on sound changes—"phonological variation"—in a stratified society points to both what distinguishes the prestige dialect and what causes it to sound different. The first point he makes is that the prestige dialect cannot be simply equated with the social elite or ruling class. He pins it down, as have Kahane and Kahane (1979), to the professional representation of the dominant economic and political culture—academia, law, business management, media and medicine. It does seem to be more helpful to define the dialect by the speakers, rather than by grammatical forms. The place and value of the standard in the occupational hierarchy is maintained as one group holds its most favored status by virtue of its ability to work this prestige form.

This does not always bode well for the alleged basis of standard English—its common intelligibility and general suppleness. Leon Botstein has recently taken exception to the effects of this economic dependence on language in institutions of higher learning:

> The faculties of American colleges and universities have, like the professions, become collectively and economically dependent on their ability to manipulate and communicate a narrow, noncommon special language officially regarded as legitimate and essential for most academic careers. (1981, p. 403)[3]

As for the prestige dialect's continuing distinctiveness, Kroch points out that "there is both experimental and historical evidence that prestige dialects require attention to speech, attention motivated not by the needs of communication but by status consciousness" (p.19). The "not by the needs of communication" would seem to reflect badly on the prominent claim of "effectiveness" for standard English, unless it were a claim to communicating status consciousness, which is not, I suppose, to be ruled out. At any rate this concern of prestige-dialect speakers makes their dialect less susceptible to phonetic change and conditioning.[4] However, they are given to borrowing from other prestige forms. These facts could be used to suggest an alternative evaluation of popular and standard dialects; the popular might well be viewed as both vigorous and innovative—in command of the future—while the standard is conservative and open only to pretentious imitation.

Kroch also provides an interesting reinterpretation of William Labov's work on phonological shifts. It would seem that Labov had been guided away from the prestige dialect thesis by his commitment to the equality of dialects. In Kroch's estimation he thus missed arriving at full explanation of his findings. (Labov, in at least being sure of where his heart lay in the matter, did not find his work used against what he stood for, as opposed to the case of Basil Bernstein which will be reviewed later in this chapter.) Kroch has uncovered in Labov's research the following patterns of phonological development: the sound change originates in the working or lower middle class and spreads outward influencing the prestige dialect, until at some point the change begins to draw some attention. At that point "a process of suppression" in the upper middle class begins and spreads back down the social hierarchy (Kroch 1978, pp. 30-1). Kroch concludes: "Labov's results indicate not only that the social elite suppresses change but also that the motivation of this suppression is a desire to maintain social distinctiveness in speech" (p. 18).

There are two major aspects of Kroch's analysis which I wish to pursue for the remainder of this chapter. Both the endowment of this language form with moral and intellectual qualities and the role of social class in the school's attitude toward standard English are what I believe to be at the centre of the term's use in school. The significance of standard English in the high school can be understood as a product of these two aspects.

The question of moral and intellectual qualities raises perhaps the largest issue in examining standard English. In spite of the references to acceptability and intelligibility within a wider international community, it is these qualities which have inspired greater efforts to champion this single language form. From its beginnings in the seventeenth century, the regulation of the mother tongue has been justified in just this fashion, with a particular regard for its moral attributes. Standardized European languages were part of the institution of a new moral order, governed, as Foucault has suggested, by a bourgeois regard for "disciplinary power" (1980, p. 105). Swift and Defoe had begun the movement in England with their claims that a standardized and governed tongue was a matter of "Purity" and "Politeness." The grammarians of the next century saw in it an escape from barbarisms, irrationality, and very unclassical-like forms of life. In the nineteenth century mass schooling and literacy were "one of the strongest of early Victorian obsessions" (Johnson 1970, p. 96). There was a moral imperative to education. It invoked a sanctity through literacy: "If (the mechanic) should be taught to speak correctly, he should be taught to act uprightly" (Ryerson, cited by Graff 1979, p. 32).

In this century the imperative remains; the ideas of Egerton Ryerson, Horace Mann and the other founding fathers continue to haunt school corridors, though their sentiments do not, as often, recieve such clear expression. One change has been an increasing regard for the issue of **equality**, while attempting to maintain the distinction of this form of speech termed "standard English."[5] A second aspect is marked by an elevation of the literacy problem a class level or two. Leon Botstein has expressed this new concern in terms of an imitative literacy:

> The current clamour about illiteracy reflects a shift from a historic interest in empowering the underprivileged, the poor and dispossessed, with the written word to a fear that the elite, the privileged and affluent have lost interest in either becoming or remaining literate. (1981, p. 399)

This elevated crisis is based on an elevated notion of literacy.[6] **To be literate** has come to represent a renewed investment of virtues in standard English as a language form. Botstein also provides a sense of just what this enhanced literacy entails:

> the ability to think and express in speech and print complex analytic and critical thoughts and feelings . . . to retain, manipulate and command complex ideas and expressions. (p. 407)

Rather than a definition of "literacy in the true sense," as Botstein claims (ibid.), it is as much a partial description of a privileged occupational sector (for example, the lawyer working on a legal brief; the professor polishing his dissertation into a book). Though it receives less emphasis, it is also a conception of literacy with its roots in the doctrine of correctness: "to become literate, and thereby to recognize correct usage" (p. 400). At any rate, literacy is no longer to be understood as simply the ability to make sense out of print, which in our society is much too universal to serve as any sort of point of distinction. This enhanced literacy entails a subscription to such notions as the doctrine of correctness, the authority of the printed text and the greater command of the world for this form of discourse—that is, a right to be heard.[7] There has been a glorification of this state of literacy—of **literate being**—much as Christianity was touted in the midst of otherwise happy heathens.

F. R. Leavis provides a most appropriate example of this tendency to glorify literacy. He has had a profound affect on the teaching of English in both English and Canadian universities, and thus on the training of teachers for the lower schools (Mathieson 1975). Language, in his scheme, takes on significance only in association with literary creation; in the study of English is to be found "the living principle." "The nature of livingness in human life is manifest in language--manifest to those whose thought about language **is**, inseparably, about literary creation" (1975, p. 44, his emphasis). It would seem that those whose life, or thought, is otherwise taken up are a pitiable lot. In considering life outside this living principle, Leavis is reminded of this passage from Lawrence's **Lady Chatterly's Lover:**

> The utter negation of natural beauty, the utter negation of the gladness of life, the utter absence of the instinct for shapely beauty which every bird and beast has, the utter death of the human intuitive faculty was appalling.... What could possibly become of such a people; a people in whom the living intuitive faculty was as dead as nails, and only queer mechanical yells and uncanny will power remained. (cited by Leavis 1975, pp. 14-15)

However, in defence of Lawrence, who had been a school teacher and a most unhappy one, he was not given to making such a very big thing out of literacy, or of schooling in general. "Teach the three R's and leave the child to look out for his own aims" is how he simply put it in **Education of the People** (cited by Gold 1975, p. x). The issue, at least in this instance, is not the elitism which Lawrence and Leavis might share--"dead as nails" indeed. It is the difference between Lawrence and Leavis to which I would draw your attention. It lies in Leavis investing such an unearthly amount of virtue and principle in a single form of life which is itself absorbed in the significance of a single language form. The Chatterly's gameskeeper, so far as I can recall, was not so absorbed.

The second aspect of standard English's endowment is its often rich intellectual claims. There are elements of this present in Botstein, but in this section I wish to place the entire issue in the historical context of the educational concern with aptitudes and the search for an acceptable explanation for inequality of opportunity in the schools and in society. It might be viewed, with some cynicism, as a series of rhetorical ploys covering for a democracy which has failed to deliver on all its promises to all its people. It might also be characterized, only somewhat more cheerfully, as a progressive movement out of racist, sexist and patronizing explanations into at least more tolerant, if not more obscuring, sentiments. It has been, then, a century of searching for the right things to say. And research has followed this rhetoric. It has sensed that where there is a fumbling concern for the right words, substantiating and professional opinion will be sought, and financially supported. The only consistent factor in this has been the relative stability and obdurateness of the inequality, even in the face of a massive mobilization of resources to make it otherwise (see, for example, Halsey et al. 1980; Mare 1981). And the only predictable result of this mobilization has been the tremendous growth in education and its numerous subsidiary operations (Husen 1979). We have always expected education to do the job. And in a certain sense it has.

To understand the current place of language in this pursuit of an explanation, we must see it as part of a larger paradigm—a paradigm which has been termed **essentialism**. This approach originated with, and proved indispensible to, the growth of universal compulsory schooling. Noelle Bisseret has located its origins in a nineteenth century concern with a justification for inequalities:

> Thus explanatory schemata were developed to account for social differences and inequalities in the very name of egalitarian ideology. Prior to Darwin and the investigation into hereditary mechanisms, a justificatory system of social inequalities on the grounds of natural aptitudes and their hereditary character was already established. (Bisseret 1979, p. 12)

There has since been a constant attempt to account for social inequalities by qualities which might be ascribed to nature. The explanation is to be situated in **essential**—rather that socially constructed—differences. Bisseret tells a touching tale of Binet, at the turn of the century, being led by the Ministry of Public Instruction into developing an instrument to measure intelligence. He had been working on the influence of environment—"the neediness and sheer poverty of large families"—as it affected the genesis of higher intellectual functions (p. 17). But with regret, apparently, he became absorbed in developing more sophisticated and sensitive tests for placing a finger and a figure on the child's natural **aptitude** for schooling. The practice of testing spread; its ability to predict scholastic achievement was particularly attractive as a screening and selection device. In the United States its usefulness was first recognized by military and immigration officials. Its potential as an educational instrument soon followed, and was principally underwritten by the large industrial foundations.[8]

As Terman saw the obligation in 1917: "at every step in the child's progress the school should take account of his vocational possibilities" (cited by Bowles and Gintis 1977, p. 197). It was part of an attempt to maintain "essential" differences that otherwise might tend to get lost in a growing universal educational system. The measurement of aptitude also represented a gearing up for a more efficient division of labor through curriculum and placement. Not to be ignored in this was the construction of essential gender differences. Thorndike, in his self-proclaimed capacity as a "serious student of human nature," advised: "The most striking feature of instinctive equipment consists in the strength of the fighting equipment in the male and the nursing instinct in the female . . . unreasoning tenderness to pet, coddle, and 'do for' others" (cited by Bowles and Gintis 1977, p. 198). This notion of essential differences was to assure that every person was in the right spot in society; it meant the most efficient utilization of resources. At the same time that the intelligence test provided prediction and place, it also offered explanation and justification; it established an essential difference on the essential question— general intelligence (the **g** factor). To convey some sense of the significance intelligence took on in the nineteenth century, Bisseret cites this definition from Laveaux's dictionary of 1830: "a certain straightforwardness of the soul which perceives what is true and just, and keeps to it" (p. 12). It is a moral conception of intelligence which has not been superseded. As Richard Herrnstein has recently over-generalized on behalf of his readers and in a defence of IQ tests: "intelligence tests correlate with so much people care about" (1980, p. 50)[9]

Intelligence testing has, of course, been an educational battlefield for some time now; there continue to be skirmishes over nurture vs. nature, cultural bias, and test validity[10]. But the central tenet—that there is an essence which can be ascertained—often remains unchallenged, but not unscathed. The amount of IQ testing and the degree of faith in it have declined. We have moved on to other explanations within this essentialist tradition. In the 1950's motivation began to serve; it was less patronizing, giving more credit to individual initiative than had genetic theories. Language differences formed the next explanatory schema, arising in the 1960's, as the dominant means of explaining inequality of educational outcomes:

> The most immediately accessable cause of educational failure is to be sought in language. Beyond this, and underlying the linguistic failure is a complex pattern of social and familial factors. . . . It is a limitation of the child's control over the relevant functions of language. (Halliday 1969, p. 19)

With notions of linguistic deprivation and restricted codes, the essentialist ideology continued to shift from a biological to an environmental explanation. It was part of a liberal solution to an apparent and continued failure to deliver on the democratic promise of equality of opportunity.[11] The liberal and professional concerns produced, over the last two decades, a host of programs meant to compensate for the ravages, or at least the unintended consequences, of life in the free world. Many of these programs have specifically focused on the "language deprivation" of the disadvantaged:

> From what is known about verbal communication in lower-class homes, it would appear that the cognitive uses of language are severely restricted . . . The speech of the severely deprived children seems to consist not of distinct words, as does the speech of middle-class children of the same age, but rather of whole phrases or sentences that function like giant words. . . . Instead of saying, "I ain't got no juice," he says "Uai-ga-no-ju." (Bereiter and Englemann 1966, pp. 31-2)

To have these giant word users ennunciate "I ain't got" more distinctly, Bereiter and Englemann would provide an earlier initiation into the institutional experience and an earlier exposure to professional interests. The implication was that the environment which particularly disadvantaged these children was the non-middle class concerns of their family. As Basil Bernstein has perceptively noted with regard to compensatory education:

> [It] serves to direct attention away from the internal organization and educational context of the school, and focus our attention upon the families and children. . . . If only the parents were interested in the goodies we offer; if only they were like middle-class parents, then we could do our job. (Bernstein 1971, p. 192)

It was quite an isolated notion of environment; with the poor set apart from the world in which the middle class somehow seemed to thrive. There was no sense of a possible connection or dependence in the relationship of the classes. It was also a restricted concept of environment, in both what it deemed to be missing--the standard English experience, for instance--and in what was beyond reproach—the entire political economy. The inherent fairness of the meritocracy was bound to be finally realized, if only reading scored could be more equally distributed.[12] The Head Start program is one of the larger examples of this approach; its failure, or at least decidedly mixed reviews, has to be counted as one of the contributing factors to the demise of the liberal solution in the United States (see, for example, Payne et al. 1973). However, in this shift away from biological and innate explanations, the legitimating function of an explanation for failure has not been forsaken. The ideological work which a field like craniometry was employed to do in the nine-teenth century was to be sustained through the twentieth by the education system:[13]

> By awarding allegedly impartial qualifications (which are largely accepted as such) for socially-conditioned attitudes which it treats as unequal 'gifts,' it transforms **de facto** inequalities into **de jure** ones and economic and social differences into distinctions of quality, and legitimates the transmission of cultural heritage. (Bourdieu 1974, p. 42)

An explanation in essences was not meant to result in a redistribution of rewards or power, but in a conviction that all is fairly distributed. The explanation begins to take on the feel of reality; it "becomes necessity and fate and is lived through happily or unhappily as the case may be" (Berger and Luckmann 1966, p. 91). It is a conviction, interestingly enough, which more directly addresses the dominant group, rather than the "victims." It does filter down, in assumptions and in a method of regard and treatment, but the ideology itself is continually worked and specified in bourgeois domains—the universities, journals and popular media. What is also to be noted is that an essentialist ideology particularly affects students and teachers, who both work within the confines of its strongest institu-tional expression:

> Students are even more vulnerable to essentialism because, as adolescents and apprentices, they are always in search of what they **are**, so that what they **do** seems to concern their whole being. As for the teachers who incarnate scholastic success and are required constantly to pass judgement on the abilities of others, their professional ethic and morale depend on their regard-ing the abilities they have more or less laboriously acquired as personal gifts and their imputing other people's acquired abilities and ability to acquire abilities to their essential nature. (Bourdieu and Passeron 1977, p. 70)

My point in reviewing this ideology of essentialism is to demonstrate that the talk of language capabilities and competencies is a reworking of the discourse of intelligence. There may still seem to be, however, a missing link in this connection among language, intelligence and essence. Basil Bernstein's work on linguistic codes has proven to be most helpful in connecting the three. Bernstein, more than anyone else in the last two decades, has contributed to the suggestion that a shift to language differences is the new best way of discussing inequality. In conjunc-tion with his team of researchers at the University of London, he has documented intellectual consequence (Bernstein 1971; 1973; 1977). To be fair, Bernstein has learned over this period to rephrase his work in much more progressive terms; he is moving away from the importance of language codes, to social and class strategies as a form of coding (1981). But what stands is his initial service in establishing this new explanation which bears so heavily on the intellectual significance of standard English.

Before examining Bernstein's specific contribution to this intellectual significance, I wish to briefly review some of the major work done prior to Bernstein on the relation of thought to language in children. The pioneering research in this area was accomplished principally by Piaget, Vygotsky and Luria. However, as we shall see, their research provides little support for the linguistic explanations and evaluations often made in education.

Piaget's position has been that thought originates independently of language; with very young children he found that thought precedes language. To explain this pre-linguistic process he employed "a symbolic function . . . which is broader than language" and is "the source of thought" (Piaget 1968, p. 91). "Language confines itself to profoundly transforming thought . . . by a more advanced schematization and a more mobile abstraction" (pp.91-2). There is support in this for the intellectual usefulness of language, at least for the middle class children of Geneva (as we are often reminded in reviews of his work). But it does not work as well for the indispensibility of educational programs in specific language forms. Eleanor Duckworth, a student of Piaget's, has noted that "there is no need to give 'language tools' (to children) in order to facilitate clear thinking . . . their own use of language will **always be adequate** for their own thinking" (Duckworth 1973, p. 149, my emphasis). Though the schools continue to revere Piaget, they cannot resist feeling the need to teach such "tools"; they do, after all, have a job to do. Thus it is that Piaget tends to frustrate educators; "either we're too early and they can't learn it or we're too late and they know it already" is how Duckworth has entitled one article on the dilemma (1979).

Vygotsky has taken Piaget to task for studying children apart from classrooms and instruction (1962, p. 117). He has, in his own research, found that the work of the teacher mediates and aids in the student's development through language, particularly as scientific concepts raised in this instructional setting is still not one of providing "language tools"; it is rather one of being introduced, if only through lectures, to more advanced concepts such as, at the age of ten: "Planned economy is possible in the U.S.S.R. because there is no private property—all land, factories and plants belong to the workers and peasants" (p.

107). In fact, the concepts lead and the language, as in Piaget, follows in this developmental scheme, though in what form these concepts become common sense I would not want to predict.

Luria's work is concerned with the regulatory function of language. He has studied the acquisition of this facility—to verbally formulate and follow a rule—from ages one to five. Children, by the age of five, were said to be able to transform control of the meaning of the words in a rule, rather than depending on impulse or adult direction—"in place of speech interlocked with direct activity, or expressive speech there developed narrative and then planning speech" (Luria and Yudovich 1971, p. 107). This and the rest of his work has been directed at proving "that speech plays a vital part in the organization of complex forms of mental activity" (p. 34). Luria's relevance to our case lies in the pre-school competency which he would establish; one that develops without formal instruction in the mother tongue. As with Piaget's work, this research does little to support the essential role schools would play in developing intellectual growth through instruction in a standardized language. Vygotsky actually concludes that the "primary function of speech in both children and adults is communication, social contact" (1962 p. 19). Another contribution to the relation of language to thought is the example drawn from deaf children. Lewis (1963), particularly, relies on this source to substantiate his claims of the general efficacy and necessity of language growth for intellectual development. However, Vernon (1968) has found in her review of the last fifty years of the literature that once the deaf sample is reduced to those who have no complicating multiple handicaps, there really are no significant differences between the intelligence test scores of deaf and hearing children.

The intellectual effects of literacy are also relevant to this question of language competencies and the limitations of the child. Research in this area has been reviewed and actually tested by Scribner and Cole (1978; 1981). They found, in studying the unschooled literacy of the Vai of Liberia, that literacy made only a small difference in specific cognitive skills—with, for example, "the ability to specify the nature of a grammatical error in Vai" (1978, p. 194). However, they also found that "cognitive skills show little generalizability across experimental tasks among traditional adults" (p. 193). They point out that while we may tend to believe that literacy and schooling improve cognitive processes and capabilities, their findings suggest that the effects of literacy and schooling are restricted to the actual practices engaged in, with only a small degree of carry-over or transfer. They conclude on both a practical and a profound note: "the research does not support designing adult literacy programs on the assumptions that non-literates do not think abstractly, do not reason logically, or lack other basic mental processes" (p. 197).

It would seem clear that the case for intellectual development through instruction in standard English cannot be easily established. In fact, much of the relationship of thought to language has yet to be clearly or convincingly worked out. But this has not prevented many from assuming the intellectual superiority of standard English speakers, nor the searching for respectable theories to back this unwarranted proposition.

Bernstein, however, in his construction of **elaborated** and **restricted codes** provided what has at times been taken to be the missing link. What had been absent from these previous studies—the role of the standard—has been the starting point for his work. Out of his experiences teaching working class students, he decided that language differences must be a central factor in their poor results (1971, pp. 2-9). He set out to establish empirically what the differences were between middle class and working class speech. As his laboratory techniques improved and his research team grew, these differences became legion— including, for example, quantitative differences in sentence length, impersonal pronouns, passive voice, subordinate clauses and pause length (Bernstein 1973; neatly summarized in Wilkinson 1972, pp. 36-7). But from these descriptive features of what he described as two distinct codes, if not languages, he was to deduce profoundly unequal and distinct world views. Consider how this was done. For instance, out of the greater use of pronouns in the restricted code, Bernstein ascribed a "lack of specification" as a general characteristic of the speaker (1973, p. 81). By virtue of the fact that the "restricted" speaker seems to favor the use of the "socio-centric" **you know**, as opposed to the use of the "ego-centric" **I think,** the speaker is said to have a less individualized sense of self (1973, p. 93). Eventually Bernstein arrived at: "where codes are elaborated the socialized has more access to the grounds of his socialization and so can enter into a reflexive relationship with the social order he has taken over" (1973, p. 140). Though Bernstein opened the world up to elaborate speakers, in a way not accessible to the restricted ones, he also disclaimed the superiority of the elaborated code. It is as if he had realized and regretted what he had constructed; in support of the restricted code he claims "not to disvalue it, for such a communication system has a vast potential, a considerable metaphoric range and a unique aesthetic capacity" (1971, p. 143). But this sentiment lacks substantiation and focus, if not conviction, in his work.

Bernstein's work does tend to fall within the essentialist tradition. His theory of codes, as with IQ testing before it, contributes to an explanation of failure located in the social group—in the way it lives and speaks. In spite of whatever else Bernstein would have, it also provides an explanation which justifies a disregard for the restricted or nonstandard dialect. It places language differences on an essential and profound level; it is not simply a question of nonstandard usage. The "restricted" child has an essential problem thinking as the school would have things thought: "the child is not at home in the educational world" is one of the ways Bernstein puts it (1971, p. 199).

This notion of different patterns of thought arising out of different language forms has its roots in anthropological linguistics. Specifically, it is to be found in what has come to be known as the **Sapir-Whorf hypothesis,** which is based on the research and speculations of Edward Sapir and Benjamin Whorf earlier in this century.[14] The hypothesis would suggest that different cultures are codified and constrained by their language. Ideas are not equally translatable into other languages; if we don't have a word for it, the idea is probably absent and truly alien. Whorf's linquistic work was based, it should be noted, on comparisons of what he termed **Standard Average European** with the languages of the Hopi, Shawnee and Nootka. But even with the large contrast between cultures, his speculations on the differences in thought have come under severe criticism.

As reviewed by Currie (1970) the evidence suggests that while there is support for the contention that language influences perception of direct natural experience (for example, color), the stronger claims of language directing social perception and world view appear to be without foundation. As Currie summarized it:

> [The concept of a] powerful linguistic influence on world views seems to be generally unfounded. A pervasive idea of an intense need for intellectual endeavor in a particular field is well able to overcome linguistic barriers. (1970, p. 418)

Bernstein has used language and cultural differences of quite a nominal sort compared to those which Sapir and Whorf were studying. He has, though, relied on these lesser linguistic differences to establish a theory which leaves thought just as tightly in the grip of dialect differences. The child has to first confront and master the elaborated code as a preliminary step not to just meeting the linquistic orientation of the school but to meeting the intellectual receptiveness or open-mindedness required.

The sort of theoretical and ideological mess which Bernstein has found himself in has resulted from extracting and detailing the differences between middle and working class speech. His codes have become so hard to handle that all his efforts to restructure this theoretical framework seems so much fumbling about.[16] For example, he has made the codes invisible—"not directly observable"— seemingly to keep them from falling into the wrong hands (Bernstein 1971, p. 15). And, similarly, he has tried to detach them from class, which in a sense further reifies them; they are now just "broadly related to class" (1971, p. 209).

This emphasis on the hegemonic effects of Bernstein's theory of codes—in its support of bourgeois language claims—is not just a hypothetical reading of his work. Like the story of atomic energy, if not nearly so dramatic or tragic, his work has been employed by both theorists and policy makers to make of language what they needed at the time and what he would deny—"clearly, one code is not better that another" (1971, p. 135)! Clearly? In fact, the instance of Bernstein for teachers I wish to consider replays rather exactly the same valuations, and the subsequent denials. Andrew Wilkinson's **Foundations of Language** (1972), is a highly-readable summary of current research and theory on language acquisition which made it a popular text for teacher preparation courses. Bernstein's theory of codes is presented in a chapter titled "Linquistic Disadvantage: Its Nature." He reminds the interested educator that those labelled "linguistically deprived" still have a linquistic competence, as he draws on Chomsky's distinction between performance and competence. However, what follows the making of this distinction is a discussion of the restricted code, with a chart summarizing 18 differences between the restricted and elaborated codes, including reference to such factors as coherence, relevance and feeling—"Restricted: communicates attitude . . . . e.g. loudness" (Wilkinson 1972, p. 136-7). Wilkinson does cite some of the milder criticisms of Bernstein, but concludes, that though linguistic terms are inadequate to define language disadvantage, "we can nevertheless agree about its existence" (p. 139). He goes on to reassure us:

> The root of disadvantage of many people is that they do not feel a **need** to develop their language, and the reason is that they are unaware of the possibilities of language. They imperfectly appreciate the nature, the uses, and the joy of language. They have a jewel worth a fortune, which can be worked to a rare edge of beauty; and they are playing marbles with it in the backyard. (p. 139, his emphasis)

I quote this in full to capture its aggrandizing of the writer's singular claim to language competence. Bernstein needn't have come to this, but he has and it is not without reason. Bernstein and Wilkinson would both ask teachers to stop disparaging nonstandardized speech, while they continue to celebrate the intellectual superiority of their own form of discourse. It presents an interesting dilemma for the classroom teacher.

Sinclair Rogers has examined the sense that teachers have made of Bernstein's theories of codes; he finds it apocryphal. He presents a compendium of views gathered from teachers he interviewed, which, he adds, were expressed with a great deal of conviction:

> There are WC and MC children coming from their respective backgrounds. The WC children have restricted language, the MC children do not. Children are proficient in one "language" only and are thus relatively unable to switch codes.
>
> School uses, society requires, the MC language so that WC children who cannot change their ways of speaking do less well at school and in society. This is self-evident. WC language also involves a different (shallower?) kind of thinking thus making it even more difficult for a WC child to be successful in a mainly MC world. (Rogers 1976, p. 20)

Similarly, Jack Thompson (1977) has found that teachers employed the theory of codes to formulate expectations about the students, and thus the theory contributes to a process of self-fulfilling prophecy (to be discussed in more detail in the next chapter). The comfort and solace which essentialism provides for education might have meant that Bernstein was bound to be picked up and abused, though I'm inclined to believe that there are elements of the ideology in his work. At any rate, it must be realized that his was not the only paradigm available.

The alternative, a specific defence of the intellectual integrity of nonstandard English, is to be found in the work of William Labov. In his often-cited "The Logic of Nonstandard English" (1973) he demonstrates that the language of black youths of New York does have a sound grammatical basis. For example, he writes out a sampling of grammatical rules for black English, after the fashion of the grammar textbook: "Negative concord is obligatory for all indefinites within the clause . . . **Nobody didn't know he didn't**" (p. 49). He also provides examples of rules that apply equally to all English dialects, thus establishing a link between standard and nonstandard where this had been denied in classrooms and society for so long. The point has come up before in this study: standard English had an exclusive claim as the grammatical and logical, not by virtue of qualities in the language form, but as a result of its social significance.

In the same essay Labov also deals with the substance of nonstandard English. But to even begin to do that he had to establish that there was, in fact, something said in the language. He had to counter the notion that "lower class Negro children had no language at all" (p. 24). It is an idea which he suggests originates out of Arthur Jensen's interpretation of Bernstein (ibid.); it can certainly be seen in the Bereiter and Englemann excerpt cited above. Labov makes his point by changing the format of the research interview from intimidating to friendly—placing it on the child's level in many ways—which succeeded in turning the non-verbal into the verbose. But that was only the beginning; through a careful analysis of what lower and middle class youths were saying it became "painfully obvious that in many ways working-class speakers are more effective narrators, reasoners and debaters that many middle-class speakers who temporize, qualify, and lost their argument in a mass of irrelevant detail" (p. 34). Labov would indeed turn the tables in this—the middle class speaker is "enmeshed in verbiage, the victim of sociolinguistic factors beyond his control" (p. 35). The example he cites at length is a comparison of two speakers on the topic of life after death. He leads us to the conclusion that while the middle class subject has succeeded in letting the interviewer know that he is an educated speaker, he is also a less logical or rational one that the nonstandard speaker to whom he is compared (pp. 37-42). It is, of course, a strange choice of topics on which to establish such qualities. But Labov's point is to prove that it can be done; that it hasn't been done before is a result of the fact that those who do such research weren't given to such questions.

Labov's work is directed at establishing an equal regard for nonstandard speech; he does so after the manner of the colonized. Nonstandard is shown to be equal to and better than standard—more English than (the) English, as it were—beating the language and its advocates at their own (intellectual) claim. Though his research has had a considerable effect on a more tolerant approach by the schools, he also realizes that equivalency of the language forms is not the whole issue.[17] Yet he has cleared away some of the inflated intellectual claims in the language issue, the better to bare its political and cultural aspects. But he also leaves intact the tendency towards essentialism.

The most effective challenge to this vision of essence, whether in race, intelligence or language, has emerged out of radical French developments in semiotics and psychoanalytic theory.[18] Their attack on the common notations of both essence and identity are sweeping and yet too highly involved to do more here than suggest the way out. Working from critiques of Marxism, structuralism and psychoanalysis, writers such as Barthes, Kristeva and Lacan have challenged the concept of the "subject" in language. We have taken it for granted—**we** are, **I** am—but in those speech acts we have also presupposed an essence and coherent existence or identity which underlies our use of the personal pronoun. This essence may be regarded as originating in God, in human nature, or in some "presence." Barthes, for example, finds in this essence the bourgeios attempt to turn "History into Nature":

[The bourgeoisie] is the class which does not want to be named. . . . The fact is the bourgeoisie becomes absorbed into an amorphous universe whose sole inhabitant is eternal Man, who is neither bourgeois nor proletariat. (1973, pp. 138, 140)

Beneath this absorbing universality, Barthes suggests, are people who have taken their cue from language, a language out of which they have fashioned an essence. The subject is, then, constituted in language. This perspective originates in structuralism; Levi-Strauss spoke of humans as not so much in control of themselves, as created by unconscious structures—language "is human reason, which has its reasons . . . of which man knows nothing (Levi-Strauss 1966, p. 252). But to the mysteries of structuralism, Barthes has added a political economy of language. He refers to "the study of the 'ownership' of the means of enunciation, something like a **Capital** of linguistic science" (cited by Coward and Ellis 1977, p. 7). The basis of this ownership is a naturalization of certain meanings which in this case support a bourgeois grip on the world—on the concept of intelligence, education and the standard language. Language participates in the reproduction of unequal relations whether between teacher and student, male and female, capital and labour.

Language is conceived as the means of forming the subject within the relationships of power. These relations, along with a sense of essential differences, are but part of the historically and socially conditioned resources in the language. Individuals draw on these resources to form an identity—to talk to themselves about themselves. In this chapter I have reviewed the considerable efforts to naturalize the intellectual and moral superiority of standard English. These efforts represent an exercise in linguistic resource management. The standard becomes, even as its virtues are sung, a means of promoting oneself. But is only begins to pay a reasonable return when those who haven't invested in it, along with those who have, are educated in its inherent value.

2
Language in the School

What is the significance of labeling the speech of one group "standard" and another group "nonstandard?" The answer begins to seem obvious: it is an easy way of concealing prejudice about socially stigmatized forms of speech under the guise of academic respectability.

R. K. S. Macaulay

In this chapter I wish to examine the possible effects of the social milieu of the school on both language attitudes and the formation of identity. I would begin by noting that both public education and standard English do not entail the sort of upper class and non-upper class distinctions which, for example, Alan Ross has made famous with his "U and non-U" (1956). There is, as Scott Fitzgerald noted, something different about the rich (which in Ross's terms is U; non-U is "wealthy"), but it may be more so in comparison with the middle class than with anyone else. Edgar Friedenberg has sketched out those qualities of speech which link the rich and the poor, and which serve to demarcate their language, if not their lives, from that of the middle class:

> The rich and poor often speak different dialects of the same language that is quite different from middle class speech; more sensuous and direct, coarse rather than vulgar; rich in nouns and sometimes verbs but poor in adjectives and qualifiers; less passive and less conditional. Evasions are objectionable...
> . [They] enjoy direct access to and expression of their feelings and senses in a way the middle class regard as disorderly. (1965a, p. 213)

These are qualities that run quite beyond the gambit of grammatical correctness; they would speak to a different orientation towards the world and, as Friedenberg has explored elsewhere, a different conception of truth (Friedenberg 1965b). Yet this shared language is beyond Bernstein's attempts to describe the restrictiveness of the language used by those who do not do as well in schools. These direct qualities of speech, as Friedenberg points out, also lead to the rich student in a middle class school being "as much beset by niggling hostility as any lower-status student" (1965a, p. 198).[1]

This niggling hostility and general social tension contribute in their own way to the school's approach to language. The general social background of teachers and school administrators provides some insight into the basis of these language attitudes. In an earlier study, Friedenberg has commented on the importance of the staff's attitudes and anxieties which are contained in the solid core of lower middle class values and folkways of the school (1959, p. 110).[2] This social class has seemed particularly given to notions of correctness and propriety in language usage. William Labov (1972a) has established that the lower middle class subjects in his study of New York residents exemplified four related attitudes toward language. He found that lower middle class speakers "went beyond the highest-status group in their tendency to use forms considered correct and appropriate for formal style"—a condition he terms **hypercorrection** (p. 126). A second feature, accompanying the first, is a **hypersensitivity** in their reaction to stigmatized features used by other speakers (pp. 129-30). Thirdly, when reporting on their **own** speech habits, the lower middle class showed the greatest tendency (of the four class divisions Labov employed) toward reporting very low usage of stigmatized forms (pp.131-2). Finally, Labov concludes that:

> . . . most New Yorkers show a strong belief in correctness in their speech, and they strive consciously to achieve such correctness in speech in their careful conversations. In all these respects, lower middle class speakers exceed all other New Yorkers. (1972a, pp. 132-3)

It is these elements—these excesses—which have for a long time given pedantic grammarians in the classroom their image, and it is these elements which would seem to be over-represented in the schools.[3]

This is particularly significant for the student in high school. The first nine or ten years of exposure to these language hyper-attitudes, which tend to dominate the folkways of the school, will not have been without effect. But in starting high school, as Labov points out, the students become more conscious of the social significance of their speech. In fact, Labov found that generally by the age of seventeen or eighteen students have attained a complete familiarity with the speech norms of the community (p. 138). The community norms will, however, have been mediated by the language attitudes of the high school in its efforts of interpret the standards of the community.

There has also been research done directly on the language attitudes of teachers. Frederick Williams (1974) has found that the judgements made by teachers on listening to speech samples of students are centred around two factors. One he characterizes **confidence-eagerness** and the other **ethnicity-nonstandardness.** From judgements on these two dimensions, teachers tend to stereotype the student and formulate expectations as to academic performance. Apparently, some teachers need only listen to a three second snip of tape before formulating an opinion of a student's potential. Teachers would seem to have developed a great sensitivity to certain speech markers.[4] The process of situating the students and forming expectations can be seen as the first step in organizing and ordering the classroom experience. In the pedagogical literature it takes on the positive form of **starting from where the child is**.

Though providing a setting for instruction, the school is equally organized around the ranking, sorting and selecting of students. These processes are the ones which are challenged by parents, and carried deep in the child's psyche, more often than the actual teaching. Evaluation has, for the teachers and students alike, a greater sense of reality. Another aspect of this institutional milieu is the need for the teacher to establish that each student does, in fact, require the services rendered.[5] Language abilities are a central focus of these attentions as the following studies reveal.

The stock placed by teachers in the speech characteristics of the student has been examined by Seligman, Tucker and Lambert (1972). They found that these characteristics, when compared to other features of students' presentation of themselves, were regarded by teachers as the particularly salient factor. In fact, the researchers conclude that a child who wrote a fair composition, had a bright and attractive face, but who spoke with a lower social class speech style would still be judged as limited in intelligence and ability.

In another study in this area, Fender and Lambert (1972) moved beyond the research concerned with attitudes shaping teachers' expectations, to capture the effect of attitudes on their students' achievement. What they found was a subtle form of sexism at work. When controlling for verbal intelligence scores, "lower more male-like" voices were positively correlated with grades in both boys and girls (p. 262). The authority of the male voice, and the lesser regard for the female appears to be a factor in teaching the fourth grade students in the study. The importance given to masculinity is highlighted by the fact that for students of a similar verbal intelligence score, language differences in "standardness-accuracy of pronunciation" did not make a significant difference.

A most interesting and most thorough documentation of how teacher attitudes become translated into treatment (often termed a self-fulfilling prophecy) is Ray Rist's study of a kindergarten class (1970)[*] . The kindergarten teacher which he observed divided the class, after only eight school days, into three ability levels—though the students were only assigned to tables at the time—without benefit of formal testing. The disparity in treatment and teaching which followed was enough to ensure that each child's place was relatively fixed over the course of the two years which Rist observed the children. Only the distance between the groups appreciably altered. The criteria for the teacher's initial, but far-reaching, decision appeared to Rist to be:

> ...ease of interaction among adults; high degree of verbalization in standard English; the ability to become a leader; neat and clean appearance; and coming from a family that is educated, employed, living together and interested in the child; and ability to participate well as a member of a group. (Rist 1970, p. 442)

This may seem like a lot of decisions to make in the course of eight school days, but as we have seen, teachers have learned to quickly make the crucial distinctions among children. Formal testing would have just been in the way; though it can, and probably will be, used later to legitimate the teacher's initial acuity.

We might conclude that language is used by the teachers to read and place the students against the standards of the dominant group—male, aspiring middle class and eagerly responsive to the institutional setting. But I believe the issue is more specific to the schools and to teaching. Teachers are not just running a public relations campaign for middle class values as is often assumed in the critical literature. When they talk about their jobs and themselves, they are not "middle class," they're "teachers" and the institution, not the "class," provides them over the years with an identity, with attitudes and values, which serve them in being a teacher. If it is a question of prejudice and discrimination, it is one to be considered within the context of institutional expectations and the exigent demands of classroom life. A professional identity arises out of meeting these institutional expectations; the sensitivities and the skills which the previous studies documented are what make these people "good teachers"—the one Rist observed, for instance, was considered by her principal to be equal to "any in the city" (Rist 1970, p. 417).

To take this a little further, many teachers have experienced a degree of social mobility in joining the profession and their own language was a prominent aspect of that climb, however imperfect in fact: "often some of the child's teachers are none too confident of their own use of the 'educated dialect' " (NDSE 1972, p.22).

Teachers would, then, be particularly sensitive to language use as a measure of social and academic position; it has served them well, and it can accurately reveal a commitment to the institution of learning—it does reflect theirs. The very process of teacher evaluation, often enough, is focused on language performances. The superintendent comes in for a morning to **listen** to the teacher and the students, as well as have a look at their written work.

Teacher attitudes towards the written work of students have been recently investigated at the high school level by Hake and Williams (1981). They asked English teachers to rate student essays that were matched in every aspect but style. The differences in style which they constructed were defined as "direct vs. indirect, simple vs. complex, wordy vs. concise" (p. 435). They created these contrasts for the most part transforming verbs and adjectives into abstract nouns.[7] They discovered that the high school teachers rated the inflated prose higher than the concise writing; the teachers also responded to it, in their critiques, on a more intellectual level, while paying more attention to the mechanical errors in the direct pieces, though the errors were identical and the intellectual substance similar. Hake and Williams found that compared to the two groups of university markers, the high school teachers were the most impressed "with what appeared to be verbal sophistication" (p. 440). In fact, the high school teachers consistently marked the concise papers lower in the four categories the researchers used— ranging from logic to punctuation.

The researchers suggest this leads to a rather mechanical elaboration of writing as a mark of competence. The perceptive student would soon realize how verbosity is being encouraged, rather than the substance and direct expression of one's thoughts. Writing and the mastery of standard English would seem, in practice at least, to be taught as something other than intellectual profundity, sincerity or directness. It may, in fact, be understood to be opposed to these qualities. Hake and Williams find the whole business most lyrically rendered in W. S. Gilbert's **Patience**, and so it is:

> If you're anxious for to shine in the high aesthetic line as a man of culture rare,
> You must get up all the germs of the transcendal terms and plant them every-
> where.
> You must lie upon the daisies and discourse in novel phrases of your compli-
> cated state of mind.
> The meaning doesn't matter if it's only idle chatter of the transcendental kind.
> And everyone will say,
> As you walk your mystic way,
> "If this young man expresses himself in terms too deep for me,

> Why, what a very singularly deep young man
> this deep young man must be!"

Some of those lofty phrases in the daisies are found in the claims the school makes for the teaching of writing. In Nova Scotia, for example, it would seem that "its prime value . . . is the fact that it is an extension of our thinking processes . . . by writing we monitor and clarify and refine our emerging consciousness" (Fraser 1976, cited by NSDE 1979, p. 1). There is the discrepancy between what would be promoted, as this instance from the provincial guideline makes clear, and what this research suggests would seem to be more likely the case. Hake and Williams suggest the problems may be "insecurity, an ignorance of how to write any better, or a misguided belief that this heavily nominal style is the only style appropriate to significant subjects" (p. 446), though they do not specify whether we are to understand these causes as residing in the English teachers or the students.

It has also to be recalled that the ability to inflate, obscure and circumlocute, which seems to do the trick in writing for high school teachers—where the direct approach will not—succeeds, as well, in many other public institutions. It brings to mind Friedenberg's point, cited above, that the middle class rather prefer evasion to direct expression in their language. An aspect of this which might be considered are the various "restricted codes" that dominate forms of discourse in the public sphere—political cant, educational pedigese or legalese, to name just a few. The speakers of such codes are not necessarily intent on evasion or obfuscation; without conscious effort, they have found it convenient, in their professional capacities, to prevent certain issues from being raised, to prevent certain things from being clearly and unequivocally stated—decorum most conveniently forbids.

Finally, to summarize the language attitudes of teachers, there is the penetrating, though most convoluted, analysis of Bourdieu and Passeron. They bring together many of the elements reviewed above in their consideration of this attitude "which orders, among other things, the structure of language":

> To take only one example, the distinctive traits of middle-class language such as hyper-correction of errors and the proliferation of signs of grammatical control are indices—among others—of a language characterised by anxious reference to norms legitimised by academic correction—for example, the concern for good manners, manners at the table or manners of speech which betray the language habits of the petit bourgeois. . . . One can see that the relationship to language is the integrating part of a system of attitudes to culture which rests upon the simple desire to respect a cultural rule which is recognized rather than understood, and upon the rigorous attention paid to the rule. (Bourdieu and Passeron 1977, cited and translated by Rosen 1972, pp. 11-2)

Though is should be added that it was much the point of Shaw's **Pygmalion** that even the highest society was quite taken, and easily fooled, by its own concern with matters of etiquette in speech and at the table.[8]

The effects of these teacher attitudes on students amounts to more than slight variations in marks, streaming or inflated prose. There is another context to be considered; the students are, not by coincidence, in their formative years. Most important for this study is their formation of a sense of self. George Herbert Mead has suggested that this formation arises out of two social factors. First, we begin to know ourselves through an ability to take on the attitude of the group toward ourselves; second, "the inner consciousness is socially organized by the importation of the social organization of the outer world" (1956, p. 33; 1964, p. 141). The influence of these attitudes and organizations, though perhaps represented in an over-socialized manner by Mead, is not limited to the family or to the junior grades.[9] While we may often consider the child to be the impressionable one, adolescence is a crucial period in the development of a sense of self and the formation of a basis for self-esteem:

> The adolescent building his appraisal of himself is therefore extremely vulnerable to the feelings and judgements expressed by the persons and institutions of his immediate environment. He is even more vulnerable than a child because people mean more to him; to a child, a cruel parent is a little like a cruel winter—a simple though destructive act of nature. (Friedenberg 1959, p. 107).

This process of building an appraisal is similar to the constituting of a self or the positioning within a discursive reality proposed by the French psychoanalytic and semiotic theorists discussed in the last chapter. There is a common concern in these American and French intellectual movements; it is to represent the individual in the throes of a process, which goes unrecognized and unchallenged as a social creation and which determines the nature of the subject.

The prolonged adolescence imposed on the young of our society contributes in its own way to the nature of the resulting maturity. It not only puts off the process, it fosters an uncertainty and self-doubt which is left in the hands of a single institution to allay or encourage. There are also friends and family to draw on, but along with the school they combine to form a pretty constant backdrop in their expectations and demands. It can be a closed, and often cloying, atmosphere in which to grow up. The term **breaking away** properly suggests how the final step is not reaching a degree of acceptance of oneself or by the community. It is, in one way or another, to be done with it, to cut the ties of that constant triumvirate, to leave family, friends and the school behind. Yet it is often more a sensation than an actuality—many do go home again. Before that and for a long time before that, young people are faced with the weight of the school's evaluative processes. These judgements may, on many occasions, run against those of friends or family, and the student may draw on this support to judge the school wrong, or just a damn nuisance. But the effectiveness of the school's judgement resides in its narrow range of lauded competencies which are repeatedly judged with the support of the dominant culture.[10] This force and formality is particularly given to judging the student as a language user.

Not all students accept the school's decisions on these matters—Friedenberg has suggested that it is both the wisest who resist, and the gentler, more progressive, school which makes this more difficult (1959, pp. 106, 109). What has significantly changed in the two decades since his study was published is just this pervasive element of gentleness. Friedenberg describes how the high school "reflects and transmits faithfully the esteem and disparagements in which the community holds its students and their families" (p. 113); what has appreciably altered is the community of reference for the teaching profession. While the social class origins of teachers has not changed significantly, the economic status of the profession has. Through an increased use of working class tactics—militant trade unionism—and an increased sense of their own professional status, teachers have moved more firmly into the middle class.

This has variously affected the social attitudes of the teaching body. On the one hand, there remain those elements tied to lower middle class folkways (shabby-genteel) and on the other, the teachers have taken their improved status to heart (if not to their tailors). The community which this new progressive element would reflect and transmit, then, might be better described by the readership characteristics of **Maclean's** or **Time** magazine, than by any given population the teachers happen to be serving. What this has contributed to is a gentler school approach—a more liberal tolerance of both the least and most fortunate students. Evidence of this increased sense of professionalism is to be found in the tone and temper of the Nova Scotia provincial guidelines. The guidelines on language contain repeated attempts to address and correct those who seem to insist on holding to lower middle class folkways, while drawing that more-than-middling salary. **Aspects of English**, which does represent quite a sophisticated linguistic statement and which still is in use, begins, with compassion:

> Understandably, the largest and certainly the most dominate group of teachers of English is represented by the . . . "what they need is to go back to old fashioned grammar" or "give us drills" school. To some extent the point of view

is valid. But a few serious limitations should be noted. (NSDE 1972, p. 5)

It then proceeds to point out that there has been proven to be "very little relationship between a knowledge of grammar and the production of well written material" (ibid.).[11] Serious limitations indeed. But, in effect, within this new linguistic savvy are trace elements of the attitudes which Labov found among the lower middle class, and which Bourdieu and Passeron reminded us "betray the language habits of the petit bourgeois." There is the reference, already cited, to every teacher "knowing full well that it is his job to do something about such speech" which suggests something more, in tone, than mere ad hoc lessons on irregular verbs (NSDE 1972, p. 5). In another section, after quite a sensitive defence of the child's family as speakers of a respectable form of language, there is reference to the useful distinction provided by Bernstein's theory of codes, and a basic tenet of linguistic deprivation:

> Some children come to school with the bare bones of language: "yup," "nope," "can't," "get up," "get out," and "shut up." From birth these expressions and others like them are the only language interactions they have had in the family. (NSDE 1972, pp.22-3)

The stereotyping of "some" children—do we all know who they are?—is accomplished here as much through their life at home as by their language. The condemnation of their bare-bones language is apt to be confounded with the moral disparagement of their family. As the teacher is appalled, I suppose, so the teacher is prepared. Though the guideline suggests an unthreatening and congenial atmosphere for the classroom, "one of the tasks of education is to lead to an awareness of the limitations of one's code" (ibid.).

In a more recent guideline, **Learning about Language** the ambivilance continues in a more strident form:

> **Teachers of young children must show absolute respect for the language of each child's home** . . . . By the end of the primary years it can be expected that children will have eliminated all babyish expressions from their language and will have begun to recognize and use the standard forms of many irregular verbs. (NSDE 1978, p. 25, original emphasis)

But can the respect ever approach the "absolute?" It would seem to defy the nature of the institution; we are not given to schooling those for whom we have absolute respect. The dilemma for these guidelines would seem to be their own compulsion to correct badly informed prejudices, while not letting their sophistication run away with the need for an instructional rationale.[12] The guidelines continually speak in terms of the children's **needs** for both attitudes and skills: the school would develop curiosity and interest with regard to language; it would respond to "local needs" in language (NSDE 1978, pp. 1, 27). "Fluency and competency in all modes of language" are regarded as a need only the school can meet, as surely as it is theirs to judge (p. 1).

However, the more recent provincial guidelines on language reflect a new mood for the new decade. **Elementary Language Arts: An Overview** (1980a) reduces the sentiments of language tolerance to a single sentence, without the previous references to diversity of background. The booklet is much more "on-task"; there are an overwhelming number of responsibilities for the teacher—to diagnose, help, share, stimulate, plan—all in the form of checklists to facilitate self-evaluation, "under the guidance of the principal." The guideline is most notable for its change in tone; it forthrightly asserts that there are now criteria, roles and responsibilities for principals, teachers and students. Yet, it is not in any way a return to grammar exercises and drills—"the Department's continuing policy [is] that language is learned through **use**" (p. 2, original emphasis).

For the student, it seems particularly important, while being polite, neat, and conscientious, to enjoy the language experiences; one third of the ten checkpoints for self-evaluation by the grade threes are predicted by "enjoy" (pp. 10-11). The self-evaluative queries for teachers reiterate the aspect of constant control through vigilant and self-conscious attitudes and responses in the classroom. The guideline does not discuss, it interrogates and challenges (cf. NSDE 1972). In a sixteen page booklet there are seven pages of direct questions and three of numbered responsibilities. **Accountability** has come to policy-making in language instruction, if not to school practices, in the province of Nova Scotia.

The making of policy, however, is an optimistic gesture, often at the mercy of the informal and pervasive practices of the teacher. Teacher regard for standard English, especially an English teacher's regard for it, is not simply another issue in curriculum to be decided, like the grade level at which geometric transformations are introduced. Standard English forms a basic part of the English teacher's expertise and authority. In considering how best to handle this authority in language, John Edwards (1979) has advised that the teacher not impose nor judge, but serve as a model in the use of the standard, which he believes will neutralize the threat to the student's nonstandard language and self-esteem. It remains a reasonable prescription for English teachers, disturbed only by the fact that the teacher's attitude has proven on occasion to be more than just an ignorance of the effects of language prejudice.

Laurie Walker et al. (1975) have tested this proposition with teachers in Newfoundland. The researchers found that the role which dialect plays in language learning could be taught to teachers through a carefully planned in-service session. Yet the general attitude of the teachers toward the local dialect was not significantly improved when compared to a control group. Walker concludes, none too optimistically that this deep-seated attitude "probably owes its genesis, in part at least, to factors other than rational, cognitive processes" (p. 9).

As I stressed above, this prejudice functions within a field of institutional expectations. On the one hand the teacher is admonished, as a moral responsibility, to accept, respect and encourage students equally, while, on the other, as a responsibility of the job, the teacher must grade, sort and document.[13] The very identification of standard English with all aspects of the school effectively blocks the notion of an equal regard for other language forms. Finally, the language form itself should not be mistakenly regarded as an object which just happens, by convention, to have a valued social significance; it has been constructed of elements which are then used to affirm or deny the social significance of others.

This more subtle attack on the student's self-esteem, through the issue of language, can take various forms. Chris Searle (1972), in his report on teaching in Tobago, cites psychologist Godfrey Palmer on the effects on black children confronted by the school's language:

> He becomes insecure and hurt when it is suggested he doesn't speak English. His immediate reaction is one of confusion, suspicion and aggression to a statement which if true deprives him of a feeling of belonging that a language confers. (Searle 1972, p. 43)

Searle also points out it is not just a matter of learning the dominant form, for the form contains a further denigration of blacks—Searle cites a black writer from a V. S. Naipaul novel: "You know, in English black is a damn bad word. You talk of a black deed. How then can I write in this language" (Searle 1972, p. 40). Not only does this make the language more difficult to write in, it equally complicates the making of an identity out of it. In this case, "black" has been reclaimed and made beautiful, but only through the united struggle of blacks creating a new resource in the language for themselves.

It is again a matter of linguistic resources. For example, there is a use of "Jew" in English that is difficult to imagine would be possible in Hebrew. "Man" in English, to consider another example, is intended, at times, to encompass women as it defines the species, and at other times, to exclude them. It requires some forgetting of what one is, in what can seem at times to be the language of others.

The concept of a standard language must be considered as just one strategy of exclusion and consolidation. Within the standard are further resources encoding the anxious concerns of the dominant to reaffirm their "right" to their position. To aspire to this dominant form means not just learning the language—the stylistic niceties and the crucial social markers—it means participation in the process of hegemony and domination; that is, one also begins to exclude others, even as one affirms one's own "right" to join the dominant group.

This point has been succinctly made by feminist research on language. The middle class has, since the eighteenth century, appropriated propriety and decorum with its prestige dialect; proper English was to be the center of their gentility and educated superiority. It would be taught to their children as part of their inheritance. Certainly, then, it would be necessary and becoming for their women to speak it, and they did so marvellously well. But the question then arises, why wouldn't similar prestige and power accrue to the women who mastered the standard form? Against this possibility other strategies were drawn on. The talk of women, in another act of appropriation, was continually denied the same level of seriousness or credibility as that paid to the talk of men. As an aspect of this there was the grammatical prescription which established the masculine as the norm and the comprehensive through the use of the generic "he" and "man". In the words of Dale Spender:

> It supports the Ardener model [in anthropology] of dominant/muted groups, indicating the way in which males can construct language so that it is a reinforcement of their identity while requiring females to accommodate and transform those usages . . . . What the dominant group can take for granted is problematic to the muted group and this could be another means whereby they are kept muted. (1980, p. 154)

It again becomes that much more difficult to fully make oneself out of a language which seems to have built into it challenges to one's sense of self. It is not just a case of unintended bias or, even more innocently, convention, as some writers will claim. It is a conscious, or perhaps it is better considered even more deeply entrenched, as an unconscious attempt, to sustain a sense of self. This is a natural enough function for one's language, so is the fact that it would do so through contrast with other identities. What is more difficult to accept are the claims of neutrality and universality made for this single language form which can be so particularly reassuring for the dominant group.

Learning to read in school can be another process of initiation and acceptance into a white, male, middle class world, with subordinate female figures giving the textbooks a family touch. The recent recognition of this has led to the integration of the stories and some easing of sex-role stereotyping. But as George Dennison so vividly realizes in his work with young Jose, the psychology of literacy runs deeper than identification with a hero of your own sort:

> A white middle class boy might say, with regard to printed words, "This is talk, like all talk. The words are yours and mine. To understand them is to possess them. To possess them is to use them. To use them is to belong more deeply to the life of our country and the world." Jose, staring at the printed page, his forehead lumpy, his lips thrust out resentfully—anger, neurotic stupidity, and shame written all over him—seemed to be saying, "This belongs to the school-teachers, not to me. It is not speech, but a task. I am not meant to possess it, but to perform it and be graded. And anyway it belongs to the Americans, who kick me around and don't want me getting deeper into their lives. Why should I let them see me fail? I'll quit right at the beginning." (Dennison 1969, p. 167-8)

Richard Sennett and Jonathan Cobb have taken the question of dignity as central to the class struggle present in American society. They repeatedly draw attention to the limits on freedom and the threat to the self as both a result of this struggle and its motivating force. Jose has come up against a singularly important source of dignity, and what becomes the issue is his sense of himself. Sennett and Cobb would interpret this as a strategy of power:

> ...society injures dignity in order to weaken people's ability to fight against the limits class imposes on their freedom.... [T]hey must first become legitimate, must achieve dignity on a class society's terms, in order to have the right to challenge the terms themselves. (1972, p. 153)

Though they perhaps give too much to the intentions of "society"—it needs a more specific location in the practices of people—they do capture the political significance of dignity. It is a prerequisite to a sense of right and enfranchisement.

What is required is a perspective on language which makes sense of how this strategy both works, and is made to appear to be less a strategy than a natural and necessary fact of social life. Noelle Bisseret, in drawing on the theory of the subject (which I cited in the preceding chapter), goes farthest in providing such a perspective. Her approach has been to uncover the sense of self to be found in language. The "subject" (the "I"), in her formulation, is constructed out of the social being of the dominant group. Those who do not share in its defining characteristics—excluded, for example, by sex, color and/or class—cannot make the same unqualified distinction between self and others. That is, to be on the outside along any dimension is to face a certain state of incompleteness. Bisseret (1979) cites Frantz Fanon's work in drawing our attention to the black sense of wanting to be white. It exemplifies this sense of an incomplete self. She suggests that "there cannot be cohesion except on the side of power" (p. 64).

Bisseret's own work has involved interviewing students on their educational and career choices. Female students displayed a sense of incompleteness and uncertainty apart from the prescribed roles. Marriage and motherhood produced interruptions and a social context which became difficult to escape. The women from the dominant class, though taking on more of a sense of agency—a stronger sense of self—still experienced marriage and motherhood as a source of disconti- nuity. Similarly, Bisseret found that among male students from working class backgrounds the formation of a sense of self was problematic. They referred less to themselves as sources of action—less in control of time of circumstances—they more often felt tied to, and marked off by, their social location—as a scholarship boy or from a worker's family. They seemed determined to situate themselves as separate from the dominated, as beyond "the less than nothing" (p. 65). What is at stake is best and most simply conveyed in that notion of "being sure of your **self**."

The psychological literature on self-concept has made a discipline out of this common sensibility. For example, Rosenberg's (1965) detailed study of 5,000 New York teenagers concluded that while subjects with low self-esteem felt uneasy with themselves—"self-conscious"—those with high self-esteem valued the degree of expression, assurance and confidence they believed they possessed. Though this does more to specify the common sense dimensions of self-esteem than anything else, it also demonstrates how central the notion of a full and articulated sense of self is to being on top of things. One of the most important sources of that surety and fullness of self is in language and through language—in knowing one has a voice that matters, and a language which will be heard. The English program, as it imagines itself to be the source of fluency, pronounces on each child's ability to articulate, which means essentially to measure up to the standard.

The place of language in education is, then, nestled in the folkways of the school. Order and propriety are the official ways of the institution and those that thrive in it seem bound to keep these qualities in mind, even among their cluttered desks. Yet it is not an oppressive adherence to the standard; the voices heard in the classrooms and corridors are relaxed and often given to kidding. Which is to say that the studies reported in this chapter should be kept in their proper perspective. Teachers are open and receptive to more than the eager voice, the standard tongue, the masculine tone or the inflated prose. So much so that only in the subtlest measures do such tendencies emerge. These ranking principles are not about to overly disrupt the daily flow of verbal traffic, a weaving in and out of ritual exchanges and moments of feeling. But at the same time the language attitudes of the teachers have such an opportunity for expression that it is difficult to imagine them not being noticed. Young people amid their casual banter are bound to be busy storing bits and pieces of the puzzle, of the sense this school and this world could possibly make.

3
Teaching English
Language in the Streams

There are only three things in the world. One is to read poetry, another is to write poetry and the best is to **live** poetry.

> Rupert Brooke (inscribed on Mr. Smith's blackboard)

Scott Fitzgerald couldn't spell. Spot his mistakes

> (also on Mr. Smith's blackboard)

The school in which I conducted the research shall go by the name of Kipling High School (as all names used in the study naturally are pseudonyms). The English department at Kipling was headed by Mr. Smith whose grade ten class at the advanced or "A" academic level (10A) was among the four which I sat in on over the course of the second term in the school year. The students coming into the school after grade nine at a junior high school would select either an academic or general stream (referred to in more formal situations as "university-prepatory" and "non-college bound"), with the majority choosing academic. The academic students were then divided into "A" and "B" levels on the basis of incoming records. The other grade ten class I observed was Ms. MacLeod's general level English class (10G). Her class was much smaller than Mr. Smith's, which had 21 students; Ms. MacLeod had close to fifteen on the register and less than ten in class on most days. In grade twelve I observed the "enriched" academic English class (12A) with 22 students, taught by Mr. Allen, and the general level class (12G) with 29 students, taught by Mr. Russell. In each case, I observed the classes for ten periods, sitting in one desk or another taking notes in earnest. Other English teachers turn up in the study—Mr. Avis and Mr. Alcott, for instance—but in this chapter on the work of the high school's English department, Mr. Smith, Ms. MacLeod, Mr. Allen and Mr. Russell are the teachers from whom I took my lessons.

There could be no better introduction to the intentions of the language program at Kipling High School than that provided by **The Kipling English Primer** and **Language for Learning.** The two documents had been produced by Mr. Smith and members of his English department. **The Primer** was written in 1977, and was still standard issue for every grade ten English student in the year of this study; **Language for Learning** was written in 1981 during the course of my work in the school. The two thus represent both the range or current intentions at work in the program and a sense of how these intentions have evolved during the recent history of the English Department.

The **Primer** provides a minimal background in the traditional areas of the English curriculum. It is made up of eight parts of speech, eleven "major errors," one "aspect of style," eight spelling rules and thirty literary terms. But there is also quite a serious break with tradition contained in the qualifying remarks which appear before the main body of the text. The tone of these remarks is, strangely enough, one of disclaiming what is to follow; that is, the twelve chapters of rules, rights and wrongs, if one is to keep these opening remarks in mind, are **not** what they appear to be:

> Modern linguists realize that in language there are no absolutes of right and wrong. In this booklet "right" and "wrong" are relative terms. By "right" we mean favored in the middle decades of this century by the majority of educated Canadians who consider themselves reasonably careful in using the English language, particularly in their rather formal communications. (**Primer**, p. 1)

This, in itself, is more than reasonably careful in its attempts at neutrality and moral relativism. It reflects the influence of modern linguistics, and the context of the **Primer** indicates that the staff was caught somewhere between the prescriptive and descriptive positions. What is of interest is how the authors, as English teachers, would claim to be doing no more than attempting to represent somewhat democratically established standards—"by the majority of educated Canadians." They are not to be considered as passing judgement in these thirty pages of prescription. This position of studied disinterest is further reiterated in the very reasons they give for the creation of the **Primer**—"because students are constantly asking for the information it contains" (p. 2; a constancy which seemed to have waned at the time of my observations at Kipling). The depiction of students as a conservative force in the school is not an unusual one for teachers to make. For example, Mr. Smith, on noting that 21% of the students had indicated on the Sentence Completion Test that English classes where concerned with grammar, responded that it didn't surprise him. They were wrong, of course; grammar, as such, was no longer formally taught. It was just, he indicated, that students were so traditional in their conception of English classes. The degree of their misapprehension of perceptiveness will be critically examined in the subsequent discussion of classroom practices.

To give some sense of the document—in both tone and substance—I wish to cite a few of the points it attempts to make, and examine the way in which language is regarded. The **Primer** essentially employs two techniques in advising the students. On the one hand it describes—"the colon is used to introduce a list" (p. 8)—and provides accompanying examples. This technique is favoured in the chapters on punctuation and spelling. On the one hand, in the chapter "Eleven Major Errors" the method is to work directly from incorrect examples: "1. Incorrect: We estimate that one out of ten mistakes are the disagreement of subject and verb" (p. 11). The "major" errors turn out to be a motley collection, ranging from the improbable—"Shirley's nose was sunburned, but now it has completely disappeared"— through the classic run-ons and tense confusions, to the inconsequential—"KiPLiNg HigH" (hand printed; pp. 11, 13). The tone is imperative and definitive: "write out," "cordon off" and "correct." There is, as well, the admonition to use the generic **he**: "if anyone makes a mistake, he [not **they**] will be penalized. Remedy: Ask yourself what the pronoun refers to" (p. 12; ending a sentence with a preposition, at least, seems to have been stricken from the annals of major errors). The remedial advice only serves to highlight the background in standard English which is necessary to take advantage of the rule of thumb—to whom does "anyone" refer?[1]

This chapter on major errors is followed by one on "Other Common Errors" where distinctions are maintained between imply/infer, may/might, and shall/will— 'say 'he shall' " (p. 16; and it seems to have been taken to heart at Kipling). There is only a single "Aspect of Style" in the chapter so-named; it is, simply, "never use a long word where a short one will do" (p. 14). However, the question of style is more fully addressed in the extensive section on essay writing. The approach used in this chapter represents something of a third technique, though it can be, nonetheless, as strident as the second in tone: "**At all costs avoid beginning your final paragraph with a sentence like this:** In conclusion . . ." (p. 23, original emphasis). Still, it does differ from the rules, and from the rulings, in one significant regard: it is **not** set up to pronounce on the entire domain of language—"this is correct"; "never say"—rather it describes the means to a specific end—the well-received essay. Just so, the chapter ends with a section on "How Teachers Mark Essays" which goes some distance to make explicit the fact that in this whole business a proper attitude is paramount. As a final check for the student, there is the query: "Is it untidy, thoughtless, and careless, or is it perceptive, conscientious and fresh?" (p. 23). The **Primer**, at this point, has stumbled onto the social significance of standard English: language conventions and prescriptions are lumped together with conscientious thoughtfulness, tidiness, and "how teachers mark." In fact, in this final bit of advice untidiness is opposed to perceptiveness, and carelessness to freshness.

The **Primer** was used in the two grade ten classes which I observed. With Ms. McLeod's general level class (10G), the first twenty of the "World's Most Frequently Misspelled" were dictated during one period as a "pre-test." The dictation was conducted after the fashion of the elementary grades: the word is read; possibly placed in a sentence, and then repeated (November 18).[2] The list ran (1) believe, (2) committee, (3) occurred, (4) pleasant, (5) principal, and so on.

In Mr. Smith's academic level class (10A), the **Primer** also became a study manual; it was the basis for a series of tests requiring the detection and the correction of errors in standard English: "1. Nobody in our schools have been invited" ("Language Test: S1"). One can see how the **Primer's** initial disclaimer might become lost and forgotten. After all, would an acceptable response to "S1" be: "For sentences one to twenty, as well as for the entire infinite set of possible sentences, there are no absolutes of right and wrong?" The assignment makes no reference to what might be "favoured . . . by the majority of educated Canadians." Language, in this instance, is a test. The **Primer** acts, post-Foreword, to define and specify language, as it will be judged and as it counts. One can begin to see the complex fabric of intentions and understanding, policies, and practice at work in a single English classroom.

Language for Learning was, as its subtitle indicated, a brief submitted to the Steering Committee for the New Grade Ten Curriculum, which had been set up by the local board of education. The brief was principally written by Mr. Smith, with assistance from Mr. Allen and three other members of the department. It is not a description of an English program for grade ten. As the brief claims, it is much broader and more radical in scope than might have been expected. It is intended to alter the entire grade ten program, and ultimately the entire educational system, with an approach to learning through language. It is conceived as a new realization of how people use language for learning:

> We acknowledge the universally recognized importance of language as a
> means of communication; however, we base our recommendations on the less
> generally recognized use to which all human beings put language, that of using

language to make sense of experience. (p. 2)

The main body of the document is only a little over three pages long. It is something of a primer for what Mr. Smith terms the "Language for Learning movement."[3] It would seem to be the form of linguistics which never quite gets out from under the shadow of the educational system. The principal figures, in this instance, are James Britton (1972), Allan Bullock (1975), and Andrew Wilkinson (1972). (It was under Wilkinson's tutelage that Mr. Smith, while on sabbatical in 1978, underwent what he terms his "conversion" to this position.) Language, through the perceptive efforts of these educational theorists, is reinvested with educational significance— the very thing the prescriptive grammar-bashing linguists had failed to do. Labov (1972b) may have demonstrated the potentially superior logic of nonstandard English, but where was one to take this in the classroom? As I believe I have illustrated in the first two chapters of this study, there are many interesting issues which could grow out of a more realistic look at language differences. Instead, however, the work of Labov and others has led to the sort of qualifying remarks prefacing the **Primer** and an occasionally uncomfortable feeling for more progressive English teachers in their role as grammarians and **arbiter elegantiae.** In this document the attempt is to throw off the traditional pedantic image of English teachers and to embrace something larger: "We are not here as English teachers . . . and when speaking of the importance of language we are not speaking of the importance of correct spelling or avoiding run-on sentences, important as they may be" (p. 2).

Rather, they are speaking of language as the "medium of most thinking in schools," a point they feel which "is difficult to exaggerate" (ibid.). They want both every teacher a teacher of English, and English (language) the centre of every discipline: "language development is no more the responsibility of the English Department than of every other department" (ibid.; they are still masters of the disclaimer). the recommendations, in themselves, are rather sweeping but mild: the Steering Committee should reformulate its discription of goals and constituent elements "to acknowledge that language is the medium of most school learning." Similarly, opportunities must be provided in the classroom to formulate knowledge "through talk" and "using writing in the expressive function" (ibid.). The **expressive function,** a term of Britton's, is central to the innovative nature of this Language for Learning movement: "expressive language is vital and rich and close to the self. It is directed to the self without a concern for audience. From this language grows our public language" (p. 2).

The developmental concept this contains raises some interesting and diverse problems. For instance, it runs somewhat afoul of the philosopher Ludwig Wittgenstein (1958, pp. 94-96). While Wittgenstein may be a little beside the point—except to suggest that a language "without a concern for audience" may well be impossible—the theories on language and development of George Herbert Mead (1956; 1964) raise a more thorough challenge to this position.

Mead has convincingly argued that it is the internalization of a public language and a concern for an audience which forms the language of the self. Even in the imaginative and solitary play of the child, which Britton and Wilkinson have so closely observed, the telling of stories to no one but oneself is still a **telling,** as if one were both performer and public and not merely involved in the play of trucks or blocks. This talking to oneself and learning to be one's own audience is not prior to going public, nor is it the vital self freely expressed. It is, rather, the actual constituting of that sense of self. It is not a private language meant only for the self, but a rehearsal and development of a public self. This sense can only be accomplished after one has gone public—entered the discursive reality—and begun to incorporate into a self what is said about one and what can be said by one. The child becomes capable of acting out the angry parent or the avenging hero, and thus begins to practise, as well as to know, what it is to be a person in the world.

Mead's theory, of course, supports Britton's notion that one learns immensely from talk. But Mead understands it as more than just talking the world into sense and organization. It is not to be seen as simply an avid, almost bookish, curiosity—this talking is a social and psychological finding and constituting of oneself. With Britton, it is as if the primary instinct, the basic drive of human kind, is to be "striking out on fresh explorations based on yesterday's discoveries": "It is a view of human behavior that makes living very like learning" (Britton 1970, pp. 37, 18). There is something too fresh and innocent, too much like school, about it all. The major difference between Mead and Britton lies in the social isolation of learning and self suggested by Britton. The theme of the teachers' brief is based on that dispersal of the social question. Language, specifically, the personal use of language, becomes primarily a means of incorporating more knowledge into the self. It is their point that this is language's great and often overlooked virtue. They have turned to Britton for a psychology of learning through language, as opposed to Mead's work on language and a psychology of the self. Britton has tried to reconcile the incredible feats of learning achieved by the pre-schooler, with the less spectacular period, often three times as long, spent in school. The approach is fundamentally pragmatic. If teachers want to enhance the amount of learning students do in their classes, the solution would appear to involve making over the vital, rich and close getting-on of infants into a school-like activity, while being sensible enough to treat it as only a beginning.

The new terminology—language in the "expressive," "transactional" or "poetic" modes—plays a central part in organizing and structuring this adoption of Britton's work. The meeting held by the five Kipling teachers prior to presenting the brief proved to be very much an exercise in using these terms, first to see how they can be sensibly used—"Is our language expressive in the same way as grade four's?"—and then pursuing the consequences of this use for school programs—"What would we **really** do at Kipling?" (December 10). It was a splendid example of providing themselves with "the opportunity to formulate knowledge through talk." But equally so, using a Meadian interpretation, this talking to themselves, in private, furthers a consolidation of their professional selves around this new terminology. They were becoming skilled at working in this terminology and its rationale, as well as becoming more knowledgeable.

Similarly, the **Primer**, whether through pages of rulings, advice in the imperative mode, or the linguistic sophistication displayed at the beginning, had spoken very much to the identity—the professional domain and expertise—of the English teacher. **Language for Learning** is firmly addressed to establishing—if not expanding, as it deputizes other teachers—the professional identity of the English teacher. That is, whatever ultimately happens to the document, and Mr. Smith said it was received politely enough by the committee, it has made its contribution to the education of these five teachers. Professional status is, after all, not merely awarded, it must be acted out and learned in just such a fashion.

That a commitment to the terminology, or taxonomy as it is referred to in this document, is very much at stake is also conveyed by a third appendix to the document. Entitled "Rival Taxonomies of Language Function," it includes a description of M. A. K. Halliday's, Jane Tough's, and Andrew Wilkinson's respective break-downs of language functions. Their taxonomies are presented without comment, except for the descriptive "rival" in the title. They would all seem to serve equally well at exposing the rather limited range of language functions and forms which are actually used in the normal course of schooling. The significant difference may well be that these rival taxonomies are wrapped up in the potential range of language functions—to predict and collaborate (Tough), to establish and maintain (Wilkinson)—while Britton's scheme is developmental. As the children grow through language, they move from the expressive function into the more public forms, from the self out into the formalities of the world.[4] All of these theorists share the educators concern with the primacy of language **for learning**, however Britton offers what seems to be a model which best parallels the school's conception of itself—taking the children out of an infantile self-absorption and equipping them for the ways of the world, with the added psychological feature of not losing touch with that self as the centre of continuing growth.[5]

A final point is to be made on learning through language, as it becomes transformed from an experience in the world to one promoted in schools. The argument which the English department presents becomes somewhat circular because it lacks any conception of why schools are the way they are. Learning is at once what everyone does with language: "the recognized use to which all human beings put language, that of using language to make sense of experience" (p. 1). And learning is, at much the same time, something for which teachers must provide "opportunities." The thrust of the document becomes this need, "which is difficult to exaggerate," for teachers to recognize the relation of language to learning and begin doing as everyone apparently already does with language. There is no explanation of why teachers have not previously allowed students to do what everyone did; there is only the admonition to begin to mirror life, where, for example, "humanity uses language in a broad range of functions" (p. 3)

What is glossed over in this attempt to mirror life is the very social stratification of language uses—particularly with written language—in our society. Consider the limited range of language functions employed in many types of work, including the teaching profession. While the streaming of courses does manage to mirror this stratification to some degree, ultimately language and learning in the school are bound to differ from that experienced by what the report refers to as "humanity." In effect, I am not convinced that having rediscovered learning through language in the pre-schooler, one can bring the process through the front door of the school and to similar fruition; the differences are not just barriers, they constitute what a school is.

There is also another element to this ambitious program which would more closely mirror life. It speaks to the hegemonic struggle of the disciplines which has been particularly associated with the teaching of English for the better part of this century. Heather Mathieson characterizes the history of English as one of taking on a "powerful sense of moral purpose":

> From its beginnings as two rudimentary skills (reading and writing) within the useful knowledge of nineteenth century's elementary school curriculum, English has come to be regarded as "coexistent with life itself." (1975, p. 11)

One can find in Britton's work, and in the English department's adaptation of it, this sense of moral imperative to place English on a level "with life itself." The material, as well as the paradox, contained in the **Primer** are not superseded by this document. The discrepancy between the prescriptive grammarian's imperative and the linguist's objectivity finds a resolution of sorts in Britton's overarching concern with language for learning. Britton's conception of writing in the school contains moments of great acceptance—in the expressive mode where one writes for oneself—and great prescription—in the transactional mode for the public. This tends to defuse the whole issue of acceptability in favour of the quest for greater and more authentic learning; it also succeeds in elevating the English teacher's concern with language from the pedantic to the truly educational, across the curriculum as it were. The Language for Learning movement offers to resolve the linguists' challenge of the standard's superiority, to make learning more intimate and personal, and as well as to re-establish the primacy of English as an academic discipline.

Much of the linguistic research done in this century—as reviewed in chapter one of this study—has done little to bolster the teaching of English in the schools. It has, in fact, debunked prescriptive grammar, as both an ineffective pedagogy and a less than credible discipline (Lyman 1929; Symonds 1931); it has demonstrated the wonders of learning and language that go on without the benefit of schooling (Luria and Yudovich 1959); and it has revealed the social basis of dialect hierarchies (Labov 1973; Kroch 1978). There was little in this work to encourge a progressive and well informed head of an English department. Enter the educational theorist, for at this point their usefulness becomes apparent. They grab the bull by the horns, and render the great body of research into a pedagogy that can work within, and generally support the work of, the established educational structures. Britton and Wilkinson have done as much with the work on developmental psychology, language acquisition and linguistics in general.[6] It only requires then, that groups of similarly enthusiastic teachers translate their work into classroom lesson plans and practices. The teachers from Kipling end their brief on just such a note, advising the committee to:

(1)   find teachers who are sympathetic to the language for learning approach;
(2)   get them to discuss the implications for their subjects;
(3)   and get them to develop appropriate approaches and assignments in the various disciplines. (p. 4)

At Kipling the position developed within this document has been specifically implemented at the grade ten academic "B" level. Mr. Smith was also experimenting with it in the grade ten "A" class which I was observing, and the other teachers involved felt it was influencing their approach to writing and language with other classes. However, it was not being implemented as a curriculum package. The program was based, rather, on the "commitment" of grade ten academic "B" teachers to, for example, provide more opportunities in expressive writing and talking:

> Today I asked my 10B's to all write down five questions they would like to ask other students in the class.... Their questions were dull.... The most common question, and perhaps it is really a touching question, was "Where do you live?" (Mr. Avis, January 5)

In the document itself the one example of student work was the response to an examination question. The question was on the novel read in class—**The Catcher in the Rye**—and asked whether the student would want to be Holden's friend. Mr. Smith reiterated in the meeting prior to the presentation that it, most importantly, shows the development of thought over the course of a page of writing. The student begins "I don't think I'd really want him for a friend because . . .," and after reviewing various aspects of Holden's behavior and attitude concludes " . . . in fact, I realize that I would like him and yes, I would like to be his friend" (**Language for Learning**; Appendix E). It does, of course, nicely illustrate the use of writing in an exploratory way "as a means of coming to grips with a problem" (p. 3). But also of note is that the student example chosen contains a very well written analysis of character. It is just the sort of answer so often called for in high school English examinations. This writing which is meant to be "vital and rich and close" continues to be focused on assigned texts in a format associated with evaluation.

That this example was chosen to be a model of "Expressive (exploratory) Writing," without a sense of apparent contradiction or discomfort, emphasizes Language for Learning's ultimate suitability for use in the classroom. These five teachers have attempted to reassure the committee that their proposal, however "broad in scope and radical in nature" (p. 3), is not beyond fitting in, rather comfortably with the tendencies of practising English teachers. As Mr. Allen expressed it in explaining the appeal of Language for Learning: "it keys in to what we are doing with students" (January 5). Another instance of this is the continued use of the **Kipling English Primer** as part of the curriculum and evaluative practices in English; it may be rewritten in "less adamant and pompous tones" as Mr. Smith assured me it soon would, but it is not about to be superseded by the Language for Learning movement (November 10).

The movement, which does intend a revitalization of English in the high school, is also something of a boon for the intellectual significance of standard

English. Though at first glance this would hardly seem to be the case. It has met the question of "Why, if there are no absolutes, there may still be a mark taken off for each standard English error?" The answer becomes, quite simply, to prepare one for going public. Yet, it still avoids, as the **Primer** attempted too, any sense of commitment to a standard. Equally so, the social significance of the form is still not considered, except that as it is the acceptable it is the necessary. However, the Language for Learning movement does contribute to a vested interest in the standard; it would revitalize the intellectual importance of the standard form. The process works like this. Moving from the expressive function to either of the public modes is construed in terms of both greater formalization of language use and greater intellectual accomplishment—one of "increasing abstraction and organization" (p. 2). So that while the movement does tolerate nonstandard forms somewhere around the centre of its language continuum, and would seem to support a less moralizing approach to standard English—"writing intended for public consumption" (p. 3)—it still retains the association among language competence, the ability to learn and the employment of standard English. This point also arose in Mr. Allen's discussion of the appeal of the movement. He said he was convinced first of all by the research; it wasn't conclusive by any means yet, though he felt it was supported by his own experience. He knew that students from an impoverished linguistic background "just didn't get anywhere," and certainly couldn't make it in school; thus language is a necessary antecedent to learning (January 5).

The Language for Learning movement has fully engaged the attention of two teachers in this study, Mr. Smith and Mr. Allen; it has become central to their concept of how English should be taught, though it is by no means all they would teach. It provides the current thrust for the department, and a small group of male English teachers, including Mr. Allen, continue to be central in its development, both within the school and in its presentation to others. Though Mr. Allen and Mr. Smith have both accepted Language for Learning as the necessary and the good, they were quite clear on the fact that at Kipling it has yet to be thoroughly implemented as a program even at the grade ten level. It had, however, captured their imaginations, and for that reason alone deserved the detailed treatment it received in the preceding section. But to fully describe the significance of the standard English at Kipling High School, the individual positions and practices of the four teachers must be more closely examined. I wish to begin this examination with the pillar of the program—literature.

The study of "literature" provided the substance of almost all of the classes; it was the only text. The term is used loosely, however, grouping as it must **Macbeth** and **The Black Donnellys** (Kelly 1974), the metaphysical poets and **The Butterfly Revolution** (Butler 1979). But to call it "reading," though more apt and accurate, is to miss what the program intends at the high school level—"exposure to good literature" (Mr. Russell, December 8). The connection of literature to the teaching of English, however, will require some development, though this lack of apparent connection is itself very much to the point. For example, the fact that the students study unawares texts which have been standardized prevents them from realizing that some of the authors wrote under different conventions in grammar and, in Shakespeare's case for instance, much less convention in spelling. They are left with the impression that literature is the work of letter- and sentence-perfect writers, with the exception, perhaps, in Mr. Smith class, of Scott Fitzgerald. It is not that there is a deliberate attempt to deny language a history or to give a truly timeless quality to literature. There does not need to be a conspiracy at work in this. But the use of standardized texts, without comment, does unduly serve our current standard and its association with quality. As well, it abets the transformation of literature into a commodity—from writing into texts—separating it from its origins as a human and historical activity.

This connection between literature and standard English, however, is not without paradox. Literature as often **challenges** conventions in language and in life. One explanation, in the form of an exemption really, for dramatic innovators like Laurence Sterne or James Joyce, is that they had to know the rules in order to break them so cleverly. This conveys a sense of initial licencing, of passing English proficiency exams before proceeding to write. The fact is that literature owes little to standard English; it is quite the reverse. Standard English has been drawn from the written record of the language. But in the hands of grammarians and pedagogues, standard English has also been used to prescribe against literary practices, based on more "refined" notions than usage. Literature owes everything to treating language as a craft, as a form of artfulness which uses language in technical feats that, in fact, play on standards and expectations.

But for the enriched academic classes there is another lesson on literature. The first "prerequisite" for admission into the enriched courses is "enthusiasm" (**Kipling High School Course Descriptions: KHSCD** 82/83, p. 11). The first lesson is of literature's awful significance:

> We hadn't taken enriched English last year and most of these people had; we were just sort of sitting there looking at one another going "What **are** they talking about?" (12Af:34)[7]

Out of an enthusiasm for literature, or at least an awesome respect, one becomes **literate**. This is the connection struck between literature and standard English for these students. It still falls short of subsuming standard English under the craft of writing; it is, nonetheless, capable of producing English teachers and other literate concerns. It would foster a discriminating taste in literature and language—what Barthes refers to as the ethics of language.[8] It is learning of literature's greatness— "Shakespeare's pretty famous" (12Af:38)—and at times actually realizing it. There was, for example, a lesson on John Donne's "A Valediction: Forbidding Mourning" in which Mr. Allen seemed to lead many of us as close as possible to knowing what literature can be:

> He's reaching, reaching for some kind of image to express their parting . . . . (Mr. Allen)
>
>> Moving of th' earth brings harms and fears,
>>   Men reckon what it did and meant;
>> But trepidation of the spheres,
>>   Though greater far, is innocent.
>
> Well . . . everything beneath the moon is changeable; while above it is eternal. (a student)
>
>> Dull sublunary lovers' love,
>>   (Whose soul is sense) cannot admit
>> Absence, because it doth remove
>>   Those things which elemented it.
>
> He's got symbols that work to convey perfection. . . . Admittedly, it is not a warm poem. . . . The conspiracy of two minds to come to terms intellectually with the parting...with no little points of tenderness or endearment....(Mr. Allen)
>
>> If they be two, they are two so
>>   As stiff twin compasses are two,
>> They soul, the fix'd foot, makes no show
>>   To move, but doth, if the other do.
>
> ...and the points of connection are all those he devises. (Mr. Allen, December 11)[9]

The points of connection seemed to all arise in that class; they were not all of Mr. Allen's devising, though he lead the way. After three years of being taught the glory of literature and on occasion experiencing it, a kind of literacy can take hold with these students through a commitment to literature: "I just think literature is important" (12Af:40). A commitment to literature does support a strong sense of literacy and a warm regard for culture. It is the basis for a competency which the enriched classes are established to support.

But it is not one as readily available to the other students. The other teachers, and Mr. Allen in his other classes, teach a kind of literature, but they intend much less with it. The veneration is missing as is the sense of participating in the greatness of a cutlure. They are left with who did what to whom, or at times, who **meant** what ... It is reading, and it is felt to be a service:

> To get them to read...for pleasure....To relate issues to their lives...to at least feel for the characters. (Ms. MacLeod, December 9)

> Enable to enjoy the author's choice of details...exposure to good literature....To find out what's available. (Mr. Russell, December 8)

> My concentration is that they enjoy their reading, get something out ot it, understanding what the author intends. (Mr. Allen, in reference to his non-enriched classes, December 9)

> The whole world knows Shakespeare is literature. (Mr. Smith, November 10)

It cannot produce the kind of literacy which the English teacher and the enriched student expected of themselves. And yet the teacher would demand just that kind of concern and would evaluate the other students on that basis—circling errors in red as if to shame them into caring. This is, I am suggesting, a good deal more than follows from the intention of encouraging "reading for pleasure."

Yet for all that, Mr. Allen did not see his enriched students as particularly given to literature. He held literature to be "a formal discipline...a specialized field" and thus, ultimately, a university major: "they have to have already decided thay their interest lies with literature and that's what they're planning to major in" (Mr. Allen, December 8). However, I found students of his with other plans, "whose intentions might be in the sciences, biology or one of the arts," to have learned that their interests do lie with literature, if not, perhaps, with the more formal matters of meter, feet or dactyls. Consider these comments on the reasons for the study of literature from Edward, a student who stated on his SCT that at twenty-five he expects to be "a doctor (resident—surgery)." He is both aware of the confidence game and quite convinced by it:

> A very time-honored question: I suppose the thing is that the great writers, the so-called great writers have some worthwhile insight about human nature that we can become better people for absorbing....the beauty of literature....It's not just words that have no relevance to our lives, but something that we can really get something out of...something that will make our lives better. I sound like

half the the teachers I've had, but I think it's true....I don't just think it's a line
they've been handing us, I think it's right. (Edward, 12Am:33)

Edward has done well to learn that it is not just a line. He conveys quite exactly
the necessary sense of literature as something of ultimate value—a sense that he
has both been taught and experienced. The influence of this sense could be found in
the literary standards he holds for his writing: "When I do write I expect it to be as
good as the things I read and when it is not I sort of get depressed and throw it off."
He wanted to participate in the craft. The use of standard English will be part of his
efforts "to be as good as the things I read." The significance of standard English for
this student, then, arises out of literature. I would not want to claim that the
enriched academic work in English is solely or even principally responsible for
this; Edward gives as much credit to the fact that his father is a doctor. At this point
I merely wish to illustrate how far a commitment to literature can go in contributing
to a sense of the self as "literate."

As a final comment on the issue of the commitment, I wish to cite the first term
examination for grade twelve enriched English. The first question is on Pope's
"Rape of the Lock." It does draw rather more strongly on the formal properties of
poetry that would seem consistent with Mr. Allen's position. But what is more
important for my argument is that this question demands that the student defend
the value or "appeal" of their selection. It is a question in which conviction is
assumed and would serve very well indeed; in fact, there is no question, no place in
the question, for anything but "appreciation." It tests the student's ability to defend
the merits of a literary extract—to participate in the production of literature:

> Write down the selection from the poem you have committed to memory, and
> then explain why you found this selection particularly appealing. In explaining
> your choice you may wish to refer to such elements of poetry as rhythm, meter,
> rhyme, figures of speech, imagery, diction, and syntax. This list is not intended
> to be exclusive: you need not restrict yourself to only these elements nor need
> you discuss all of them. You may also wish to justify your choice in terms of its
> meaning and ideas. (Mr. Allen, 12A)

There is still another element which serves to distinguish the preeminent
literature class at Kipling. Mr. Allen's preference for the intellectual content of
literature shapes the particular significance the conventions of standard English
and literacy take on in that class. The importance of this preference is reflected in
the issues which Mr. Allen addresses in literature, but equally so in his concerns
with the students' writing. In the enriched grade twelve English class both teacher
and student agreed that the students have mastered "the mechanics" of the
language. "Most of them have no trouble with the obvious things that young

writers have trouble with" which, in Mr. Allen's terms means that "they have the ability to make their language useful to them" (Mr. Allen, December 8).[10] This ability can, on occasion, be guided by quite unexpected conventions: "I try not to use that much punctuation . . . the lesser you use, the better off you are" (12Af:34). But, more commonly, they are felt to have problems with conventions of another sort than those governing punctuation:

> You just forget about all of those mechanics. The comments [on the students' essays] are about, sometimes they're about style, more often about organization, clarity of your thinking, backing it up, geting rid of any confusions. (Mr. Allen, December 8)

The response to literature remains in the enriched class, as it is in the other classes, a vehicle for teaching and evaluating the use of conventions in language usage. The difference for this enriched class is, however, that sentences are marked "awkward" instead of "not a sentence." Spelling mistakes are still circled but it is understood to be a gentle reminder—not "up to half marks off" as in the general level grade twelve class.[11] On the other hand though, it is the ideas and the style of argument which are at stake in the enriched class. Still the risk is great; an entire essay can be dismissed—"He said my essays were wrong" (12Af:40)—because it is too given to hammering away—"short exclamatory sentences [where] everything sounds like a clarion blast from the soap box" (Mr. Allen, December 8). In the enriched twelve class, the concern is principally with fashioning an argument out of literature and literary convention.

In the other classes, including to some extent the academic grade ten class— "spelling and punctuation [are] absolutely appalling . . . They lack the politeness of language" (Mr. Smith, November 10)—the hurdle, the first focus of concern in writing, remains "the mechanical":

> Say I write something, just little errors, say I write something like, "I must **of** been," they would correct it—"I must **have** been." (10Gm:93)

> Whenever you write langauge, they always looking for these little mistakes, like if you spell "their," t-h-e-r-e. (12Gf:15)

> When I'm writing I try and make sure it's perfect, cause I don't like [it] coming back with all these errors. (10Af:54) [12]

Mr. Smith has begun moving against this over-riding concern; it is at the heart of Language for Learning—expression first, the politenesses of public forms subsequently. With the grade ten academic class he experimented in various ways with shifting the emphasis from "communication" to "sorting out thoughts." It is an approach that will be further assessed in this chapter, but at this point it is sufficient to point out that the shift avoids this dichotomy between intellectual and mechanical concerns without quite bridging it. For example, "The Problems of Childhood" and "Idealism Lost," two of his new exploratory writing projects (in which mechanics were not to be worried about), were evaluated on grounds of student "involvement" in their writing—a commitment to literacy of another sort.

Literature was to be used in the Language for Learning work as a point from which to jump off into an exploration of one's self, eventually to return, with greater empathy, to a study of "character" or "theme." Mr. Smith, Mr. Allen, and two other male teachers, "with" Ms. MacLeod, did produce "a sequence of 10 40-minute lessons" entitled "Language for Learning: **The Learning Tree**." They used it at a workshop to give a concrete example of the movement's approach to literature using Gordon Parks' novel **The Learning Tree** (January 25). The writing assignments in this model move from "an expressive piece dealing with what each student felt and thought about the problems of being young" to, after ten lessons, "a classificatory essay on Newt's coming of age."

In Mr. Smith's classroom the students, on one occasion, after writing out ten lines of poetry they had memorized, were asked to put down "informally . . . what you find impressive, or why you learnt them" (November 10), and on another to do a piece "on your favorite character [in **Arms and the Man**] so that a colleague could appreciate your feelings—name the person" (February 2). Literature is to become the focus of a slightly wider range of writing under the influence of Language of Learning (cf. Mr. Allen's exam question cited above). There is a greater encouragement of a personal response. As the students begin to write from this self-centeredness, and then into literature or into the world, they are imagined to be doing so with greater conviction and commitment because, the theory suggests, a vital link between the self and writing has been established. Out of this commitment and desire to express one's **self** to others, this theory supposes, will come the need "to enter the public domain"—that is, to employ standard English. From this cultivation is to follow both more authentic learning and more sophisticated forms of expression in either the transactional or poetic mode. But more than that, they turn to it for conviction:

> What we're doing in grade ten is trying to get access to their own language, so that eventually they can write about it and can write about it with conviction, so they have some relation to their writing (Mr. Allen, December 8).

But in the two general classes neither expressive nor intellectual concerns were realized very often in class. Whatever the real variations in familiarity with, and interest in, proper usage between students in the two streams, this difference played a central role in shaping the curriculum. It is as if these variations could be assumed to apply equally well to intellectual concerns and the desire to mount an effective argument. At any rate, this might be seen as the lesson they were being taught. Compared to the statements on writing of the three students cited above, the enriched twelves were concerned primarily with the coherence and cogency of their expression:

> I don't seem to be able to get my thoughts out. I try something but it doesn't come out right. . . . I should think things out more clearly. (12Af:34)

> I stink at writing. Everything comes out all jumbled, like . . . the way I talk is the way I write. It isn't organized. (12Af:38)

> If you're doing what I'm doing right now—babbling on—you sound like an idiot. (12Af:40)

She didn't sound like an idiot, of course, none of the students did; but she has become sensitive to the issue on that level. She understands something more is expected ot her than just correctness. The classes are being differently encouraged and made sensitive to different aspects of themselves. The general level students are saddled with the subject of their indifference, "correctness"; the others graduate into developing their argument. They are not just enriched but also empowered by successful teaching at the enriched level. The general level students, if successfully taught, will stop being so "careless":

> [They're] doing exercises [in grammar] very well, but they don't transfer it. They look at it in a vacuum: "You know what I mean, Miss!" They're just careless. (Ms. MacLeod, December 9)

Is it a question of whether you can discuss with students, who are still mastering the sentence which does not run on, what the options are when all about you are given to deception, or what it takes to test the loyalty of someone offering friendship (12A: **Duchess of Malfi,** February 10; **Macbeth**, January 12)? Mustn't they walk before they dance? The fact is that the general students did get headlong into the intellectual and moral content of the books; they took it beyond the text and into the morning radio news and afternoon television dramas. The difference is that it doesn't come up as much.[13] Thirty per cent of the general level grade ten classes I observed included work on the run-on sentence, just as one section (out of five) on their examination requires that they find errors in word usage and correct them (November 23). Nonetheless, Ms. MacLeod and her students did spend a month of classes, off and on, discussing **The Black Donnellys**—the Donnellys' wiliness, their barbarism, the limits of their culpability and the morality of their murder: "Well, see the Donnellys had no business being on that land; there was other good land ... and they feuded" (student, December 10). The students brought to bear on the story a recent police murder trial, the soap opera "Texas," and a local break-and-entry shooting: "It's like if I walk on his back lawn, can you shoot me?" (student, January 10). But the discussion was so easily shattered; questions of attendance, attentiveness and authority kept intruding. The discussions mentioned above, for example, developed out of the taking up of tests (December 10; January 10). In the teacher's estimation the moment of motivation must be kept close at hand. Though Mr. Allen's extended discussions with 12A across the hall might be viewed as directed towards or driven by a similar extrinsic motivation, there is just a greater willingness to suspend disbelief in that class devoted to literature. Still, in those special moments in Ms. Macleod's class, there was the use of that key to literary criticism—textual reference—and there was no less conviction or commitment to the ideas at hand; they can pursue a point with each other as if it were the only game in town.

The principal of Kipling High School told me with a measure of pride that they had achieved in the last few years a remarkably good match of teacher to academic level and grade (January 12). It is difficult to know how far such an administrative sense of well being should be taken. There had apparently been complaints a few years ago concerning the quality of teaching an honours course was receiving; that situation had been rectified and there had been no problems since. An institutional act like "ability" streaming would, more than anything else, seem to dictate what to expect—it provides the roles and it becomes difficult, for example, to imagine these four teachers teaching other levels. Yet was it a matter of a proper fit, or of their fitting? Of course, they taught other classes; though neither Mr. Smith nor Mr. Allen taught a general level class in the year of this study, Ms.MacLeod did have an academic "A" grade ten and Mr. Russell had two regular academic elevens. However, there was still reason to specifically identify Ms. MacLeod and Mr. Russell with teaching at the general level. This was to prove to be a very serious and sensitive issue at the school. Mr. Smith declined to comment on the rationale of the class assignments. There certainly seemed to be no question of rotation, or merely the expediencies of timetabling and other subject responsibilities.

Mr. Russell told me that nobody had wanted his class—12G—five years ago. It was only now that some of the women were showing an interest in it, because, he explained, the students are so much better behaved that the grade ten general level students (November 16). Ms. MacLeod, for instance, expressed an interest in his class, but said it was just assumed to be Mr. Russell's corner. She had begun at Kipling some years ago with four general level grade tens. She felt she'd had enough and asked to be relieved of general level tens". . . and I've still got one" (December 9). But she had been given an academic "A" grade ten for which she sounded grateful (December 9). Still, she has come to see something special in the general level students. They "show deep feelings . . . more honesty"; she felt they trusted her and she felt more relaxed with them—"they won't question." But like these students she taught—do they teach each other in this?—she understands that there is too often something senseless and perfunctory about the English classes with the general level ten. She had tried different ideas with them—journals, their choice of books—but it always came back to, she suggested, "watered-down academic"—a story with questions at the end (February 15). I almost mistook her "What in Christ's name am I doing here?" to be her own response to teaching; she had meant it to indicate the question that seemed to be nagging many of her students.

In her class what they appear to be most honest about is a lack of interest—they fold up their arms and put their heads quietly down. They do not attend regularly; "you cannot expect them to show up." She had arranged to have one student, who was consistently late, removed from her class. The vice-principal ruled that he must now leave the school each day at noon—a social exile. The incident which set it off was just one more late, but one more late acompanied by surliness—"rude manners . . . Bob does what Bob wants to do" (January 19). Mr. Russell told me of how he also built up cases on the tardy and the irregular (January 13). Attendance—bodily presence—is given a particular documentary reality in the school; they record it in every class. It is one of those points on which the school takes itself very seriously.

This lack of student engagement tends to be met with a certain kind of lesson—a one-shot affair, demanding highly directed and somewhat mechanical responses:

> Paragraph 1 (Setting): It was a typical night at the Long Branch Saloon.
>   A. Write a sentence describing what you see.
>   B. Write a sentence describing what you hear. ("A Story of the Old West": 12G, February 8)
>
> [numbered sentences on the board] 1.   What are the uncle's reactions to the snake? . . . ("The Snake": 10G, February 2)
>
> Identify if the sentence is **choppy, run-on, incomplete** or **okay**. . . . Check it if it's right, "x" if it's wrong. ("Grammar Review": 10G, February 15)

The marking scheme becomes crucial, elaborate and the focus of concern; it is what counts:

> Put down the mark you **think** you'll get. Exchange your books.... You'll get 20 out of 20 in December. (Ms. MacLeod, November 18)

> You score 5 points for each misspelled word you underline. On the other hand, you lose 10 points for each correctly spelled word which you underline. ("Spelling Bee": 12G, December 11)

> For each right answer give yourself a 1/2 point; that's one in each and an extra in number four. (Ms. MacLeod, February 17)

It is these elements, in turn, which determine what literature and language are going to mean in the classes, these elements as much as the conceptions of ability levels and language resources which underpin the streaming.[14] Both students and teachers have settled on a lower level of giving and of commitment, because they have been disappointed—it is to be bored, then, rather than hurt:

> 14. Students in the general level English classes—don't have much imagination or insight neither do their teachers. (10Af:55)

> —don't get very excited about their work or literature. (12Af:40)[15]

"Enthusiasm" was, after all, the domain of the enriched. Ms. MacLeod said repeatedly when comparing the two streams that the academics just want to please the teacher; it was intended to reflect on the greater authenticity of the general level students. Yet the academic students displayed a certain faith in what they were up to. If anything, they believed too much in literature, more for instance, than they probably have experienced.

The academics were also **expected** to be faithful. A student in Mr. Smith's class related an incident to me—certainly in an effort to get even—about how Mr. Smith "took an absolute fit" over a comment scribbled on the cover of her "Thought Book." She had written "I can't stand English—Blah." As she reported it, he called her into his office and acted terribly offended; he's never heard of such an awful thing—he'd thought they'd had an honest relationship (February 15). It was a kind of betrayal, not just to have resisted Mr. Smith's charm as a teacher—a match for Mr. Allen's grandiloquence—but to have been selected for an academic "A" class and to not appreciate English, that too was a crime of sorts.

The school responds to this detachment displayed by general level students in kind, or at least meets then half way on the matter. For example the school day begins with the announcements read by the "Head Boy" or "Head Girl":

> Good morning, today's announcements are as follows: Liberal Party meeting at

. . . all members **must** attend. . . . The school trip to France will . . .

-"Bonjour!" (Heckler: 12G)

. . . . The Christmas Decorating Party has. . . . Do not, I repeat do not take the word of a classmate on when and where the exams will be. . . . Take your exam results seriously and work with more dedication in the second term [the principal's contribution] . . . to be elegible to obtain a scholarship you must apply to the University of Guelph. . . . And the student of the month is . . .

-"Me!"
-"Who cares."
-"Hey, he cheats!"

. . . and as well he is the president of the Kipling Ski Club. (something of a composite collection: 12G, November-December)

It is a kind of isolation from the life of the school which leaves them, or at least some of them, with their jackets—their winter jackets—on in the class. They are not at home; they are not here to stay. Mr. Russell and Ms. MacLeod are, with these general students, dealing in grammar exercises and "gang novels"; they are dealing in lates and truancy; and they are thus themselves no longer fully engaged in the literary life, such as it is, of the school. When Ms. MacLeod decided to go to the stage production of "Scrooge" with her academic class, she told her general level ten class to "go hide" for that period; they hadn't shown much interest, nor brought their ticket money (December 8). The general level teachers risk becoming isolated if only through association with this other element in the life of the high school. These classes didn't go to the theatre events; they weren't involved with the students' council, the school newspaper, the awards and scholarships. "I've been around here for fourteen years and it's about time the newspaper got to me" is the opening quote in a **Kipling Times** article on Mr. Russell and the English as a Second Language program which he teaches. Mr. Allen, in the same issue, is "Teacher of the Month." ("Do you have any moral tidbits to offer the students? Yes, don't waste your time in High School.")

Teaching general level classes is perhaps enough to encourage a kind of resentment in the teachers, a further disassociation from these students and an exaggeration of what they, as teachers, face with a general level class. It also arises out of what they face in becoming general level teachers. Ms. MacLeod spoke of breaking out of this designation; Mr. Russell saw it as something he had made comfortable for himself—he knew how to "handle" them and I'm not sure he aspired to a more literary environment: "My pronunciation is a little off; I have to watch it. You forget" (December 8).

Exactly what general level teachers do come to understand about their classes was made most clear in a city-wide English workshop, "On the General Program," which Elenor MacDonald gave (January 25). She had just completed a research project on teachers' views of the general program in Nova Scotia (MacDonald 1981). She found in her study, for example, that practically all of the 253 teachers she interviewed considered the program "a dumping ground" (p. 52). This was the starting point for the workshop and generally set the tone: "We don't have a lot of control over who we get or how we get them." She demonstrated, through a statistical study of school retention rates in British Columbia, that 45% more students remained in high school than in 1959. General level teachers were obviously faced with students who "ought not be in school"—"a fact of life for us" (referring to Mr. Russell, Ms. MacLeod and the other teachers at the workshop, noticeably over-represented with younger and female members of the profession).[16] Ms. MacDonald provided us with characterizations of "general course people":

> your worst hypocrites . . . Archie Bunker types . . . and again the prejudices they carry are incredible. . . . The need to be part of a group is really "general" [but] for your general kids you have to select [groups] well.

She also mentioned their tendency to keep their jackets on. It turned out to be a widespread practice and was regarded as a fair baromenter for integration; it was considered a measure of success to have them de-jacket, that they might be less insulated from the entire process of schooling. The workshop ended with her dispersal of a large and desparate package of photo-copied material—old adverments, record reviews, word puzzles, and problems—that might "work" as we "try to do something with these children." Ms. MacLeod told me afterwards how right Eleanor MacDonald had been. She does seem to have hit on the lessons learning and the attitudes forged in being assigned to "the dumping ground."

There were, of course, elements which were common to all four of the classes. For example, what does get dreamt up for each of the classes, does get on the exams; or is it, as much, the reverse? There were no longer province-wide examinations in grade twelve for teachers to teach to, as there had been in the 1960's. The difference however is more of the authority of the teacher's perspective; the teachers were now teaching to their own exams. It essentially means that the student can be even more sure of the authority of the teacher's reading and presentation of the text. Mr. Allen's forty minute lecture-discussions with the enriched grade twelve on the multiplicity of deceptions—in hidden pregnancies and disguised pregnancy tests, in spies and counter-spies—within Webster's **Duchess of Malfi,** or of love, maidenheads and sexual imagery in Donne, can still be seen to have the controlled shape of an exam essay (as well as introducing sexuality, as a topic, into the class—itself a kind of privilege). In the general level grade twelve Mr. Russell's mimeographed poetry assignment for one evening was strangely headed "K.H.S. English 12G; 1 1/2 hours; February 1976":

> Value 2 (a) Why does it seem that the shark knows the harbor?
> Value 2 (b) What is the "piece of sheet iron?"
> Value 3 (c) In your own words describe the shark as seen by E. J. Pratt. . . .
> Value 1 (g) Who wrote the poem "The Shark?" ("The Shark": 12G, February 8)

The examinations themselves do serve to distinguish the levels, but not thoroughly. The general level ten examination had a dozen or so "comprehension" questions on a newspaper article, twenty faulty sentences to correct, three short story main ideas to explicate and finally two essay questions. The enriched twelves were left to concentrate on three essay questions in the same hour and a half time period. In light of these demands, consider whether these two exam questions differ more in tone than in substance, the first from the enriched grade twelve and the second from the general level grade ten:

> Miller has said, "**The Inside of His Head**" was the first title . . . and the inside of his head was a mass of contradictions." Regarding the play as a whole— memory sequences, dreams, speech, and present action—what judgements about Willy do the presence of these contradictions lead. (Mr. Allen, 12A)

> Explain fully the significance of the title **That Was Then, This Is Now.** Indicate in your answer who says it flrst and to what does he refer when he says it. Also, tell who says it by the end of the novel and to what does he refer when he says it. In both situations, something is lost; be sure you explain what is lost in both cases and why it is lost. (Ms. MacLeod, 10G)

What will probably be lost for the student in 10G are these more serious questions that need time, and that require a sense of belonging to what are sometimes called viable concerns. Have the concerns had a chance? Has the student finished finding the twenty errors in the grammar section? But of course there is another element at work here. The exam serves to prevent the gearing of class work to the student's "ability level" from fouling the selective function of public education. At least two students in the enriched academic class had sensed this difference between streaming and grading:

I was sure I was going to get like a 60 or 70; I just freaked when I got 80. . . . The exam was hard by the marks were good, I was really surprised. (12Af:38)

I was afraid to take enriched last year cause I though it was really hard and then I made 87 in this one [exam] which is ridiculous. It's not hard. (12Af:40)

The original differences in marks are for the most part about to be maintained (the teachers, for example, expressed disdain for academic student "slipping" down to the general level to more easily pick up high marks).

The enriched exam, in all its concentration, is set to match those periods the students spent as philosopher kings arguing about the who and how of guilt and motive. Literature has provided the spectacle of superhuman lives which they learn to peer into, to challenge and to judge. The lesson is a simple enough one for the enriched academic student: We are here to evaluate, to build our case, to find our precedent in the text and to take up a well-armed position. There is an authority and a sense of importance which arises out of dealing with what are regarded as the highest cultural forms. There is equally so a moral authority which develops out of the ability to argue the significance of these literary lives. An expectation of themselves must arise as they search out the contradictions in characters and apply principles, moral and otherwise, to the actions of these paper figures. "To help students in their exploration of moral values" is the final, if not the ultimate, goal of the department (**KHSCD** 82/83, p. 10). This exploration is not completely missing from the general level classes. But as with the examination, there is much—the basics of punctuation and punctuality, for example—that gets in the way. The moral focus, of judgement and censure, is more often directed towards their language and behavior at the general level, than towards literature: "This course is for students with considerable problems with using language effectively" (the complete course description for Ms. MacLeod's 10G, **KHSCD** 82/3, p. 10). Their rather marginal participation in the argument of literature, and in the life of the school, is part of their preparation of the world. That this is believed to necessarily follow, from the inability to match-up tenses and spell, marks, at least in part, the significance of standard English for these students and teachers.

"To encourage creativity in students" the English department offers "active encouragement to enter" three literary competitions and "an annual magazine of poems written by students of this school" and edited by the staff (**KHSCD** 82/83, p. 10). The announcements of the national competitions were on most of the classroom bulletin boards. Mr. Alcott had in his Writing Centre/classroom a hand-printed poster which prompted "**You** can **write** for money and fame." Kipling students had won at least twice in the national short story competition sponsored by a trust company which paid three hundred dollars for first place.

During the second term, the two academic classes submitted short stories to their teachers. I didn't happen to sit in on any of the lessons or discussions on their writing; there were only references to approaching deadlines followed by, after the deadlines had passed, apologies for not having the short stories marked. Mr. Russell and Ms. MacLeod included letter and resume writing as part of their programs. They both considered it as a particularly relevant topic, providing, in a way other aspects didn't, what they believed students could use. Ms. MacLeod, for example, felt the exercise at the grade ten level was good preparation for seeking a summer job. Mr. Russell made something of a contest out of it—as it would be in the job market.

He provided the students with a page of classified advertisements for general clerks and office help. The students were to write a letter of application; they were "to sell themselves." It had to be based on their own experience with one poignant exception; they could claim to actually be qualified for the work—with a business diploma, for example. "He said to sell yourself. I did . . . [pointing to the letter] that's all wishful thinking" (12G, November 16). The letter which Mr. Russell picked as the best—"got the job"—was done by one of the business students taking Mr. Russell's class.

> -"She had it typed."
> -"No wonder!" (students, 12G)

> Look at this, some of you only gave me two lines [hers is two solid pages]. . . . I marked for general readability. I'm sorry for putting red marks . . . [some were] more attractive; it was content plus format. (Mr. Russell, November 16)

He told them to keep the clippings; they would be doing it again. He mentioned after class how appalling some of them had been; they wouldn't have had a chance. The students may well have understood as much. They may also have realized the questionable relevance of the exercise: "For most of them [jobs] its just show up and can you do this? They give you a little talk and they fill out your information sheet and no resume needed really" (12Gm:19).

But the lesson did tap a vital concern. So vital, in fact, that in talking to the students I found a single vocational event was felt to be the sole underlying value of instruction in the student's mother tongue—the job interview:

> When you go for an interview they want to know, to see, if you can speak the right language. (10Gf:88)

If you go for an interview for a job, you make sure you try to use these words, right? Show that you know something. . . . By the way you speak, they know you didn't do that good in high school. (12Gf:15)

When you go for a job interview, if you talk very well they might think that you know what you're talking about, and that you paid attention in school. (10Af:56)

The students need a reason and this projected half-hour in their lives—though it may well get replayed—would seem to be it. It may be quite a realistic appraisal. But then the tale hangs by such a thin thread and what it tells of language is little more than "social impression management." The doctrine of correctness becomes a fashion of compliance and an expression of a willingness to be schooled. It is a long way from participating in the rich literary heritage that makes English such a vibrant tongue. It is nothing more than, in these instances of social realism, "not to sound dumb."

Mr. Smith's Language for Learning work would strive to achieve another sense of relevance with the students—not pertaining to what they would become, but to who they are. That it can achieve as much, even with the experimental and haphazard introduction it has received in the academic grade 10 class, was attested to by eight students on their Sentence Completion Tests (SCT): "24. English classes are concerned with—helping you express your feelings and discovering who you really are" (10Af:70).In response to an item on self-clarification, six students referred to the usefulness of writing:

38. What has made my life clearer to me—is the writing about myself that Mr. Smith got me to write. (10Af:66)

—in writing I have come to terms with things I couldn't deal with. (10Af:67)

Mr. Smith had been quite proud of these results. It is, when you consider it, so much more than a math teacher, for example, could expect. (This pride points to, rather exactly, the sense of a revitalized role for English in the curriculum which is discussed in the first section of this chapter.) However, this acclaim was opposed by one of his students, who resented what she understood to be at stake: "36. I might make my feelings known more if—the English teachers wouldn't pry into your life" (10Af:67).

The class has not abandoned the regular or "transactional" sort of high school assignments; there is still a strong evaluative context surrounding much of the writing. Though he claims the students don't realize it, Mr. Smith mentioned that he recorded considerably more of their "transactional" than their "expressive" writing for their term marks (January 10). The actual evaluation of the "expressive" writing is based on the level of sincerity and the degree of personal exploration achieved: "truly engaged or off the top of the head," is how Mr. Smith put it (January 25). The students are not, in this expressive mode, to be writing for the teacher, but simply for themselves. It cannot, of course, be quite that way; it is not merely a matter of perfecting the techinque of teaching in this mode. Rather, there is very little that can go on in a classroom that is just for yourself:

> This is to be done in a relaxed manner. . . . Don't worry about spelling or punctuation. I am going to mark it but don't worry. . . . I don't want you to talk to anyone. . . . I just want you to write for, well, it won't be thirty minutes now, for twenty minutes. (Mr. Smith, February 2).

This question of evaluating and thus encouraging self-revelation is a ticklish one for the movement. It was, for example, the thrust of the sole challenge to this position at a workshop on "Language for Learning" given by Mr. Smith, Mr. Allen, Mr. Avis, and Mr. Alcott. The question raised was, "To what extent do you have the right to pry; I'm not the student's psychoanalyst?" (January 25). Mr. Allen, however, recognized the challenger as an exponent of drama and quickly brought the issue into another confrontation of dogmas: the Heathcote drama approach versus Language for Learning. Heathcote offers the student a protective guise or role, through drama, with which to distance the burden of exploration and awareness (Heathcote 1980). Language for Learning allows for greater self-exploration "with a trusted adult." There was tittering among the teachers when one of them mentioned with a smile how risque some of the students' work had been; they weren't afraid of opening up for her. The therapeutic position—as far as it calls for the client to "open up" to the professional—is difficult to deny:

> I don't think of it as therapeutic. I think of it as their using their own personal experiences. . . . Because they know something about them I can be pretty sure that they'll all be able to deal with that sort of thing and they won't be scooting over the surface as often happens in their writing—it doesn't interest them if it doesn't involve them. . . . The other thing is that they've got to have a good sense of—God, I hate these phrases cause they sound like the [19]60's—of themselves and what their thoughts are of themselves, rather than just mouthpieces for what they've heard, or picked up with their ready-made phrases and ready-made ideas. (Mr. Smith, February 15)

This confusion of ends—psychological and intellectual—may be unavoidable and not unwarranted; there is certainly room for the notion that greater depth, originality and penetration in writing are only achievable through a greater involvement of the self. But in shifting the focus in the English class to more authentic and personal expression, it might well sound like the loosening up of the 1960's, except for the fact that the social awareness and concerns of that period are missing. Language for Learning, after all, arose in the early 1970's and, by God, the phrases sound like they belong to that age of narcissism: "it makes you in touch with yourself" (10Af:54, "ready-made phrases" indeed).

The therapeutic aspect, which Mr. Smith would rather not think of it as having, also matches that decade better, though in a very particular sense. It is a therapy which would use a greater self-involvement to elicit a greater commitment to the task at hand. Whether employed by corporations or schools, it is intended to produce a better performance. The revelations may be incidental, for it is the involvement which is crucial. Yet is it to be a greater involvement in writing or in the school? When I asked what might come of this writing, Mr. Smith responded that it was a real possibility that the next teacher might not carry through with it. He was concerned about this, though he hadn't yet "thought it through." When I pushed the point to whether he had considered its effects for life after school in a more absolute sense, he replied with a rather emphatic "no"; though the student's future in the school might be a concern life after school was hardly relevant (November 10).

This is to consider the program in principle; in practice another element of involvement emerges. Mr. Smith's written comments in the margins of the students' "Thought Books" were of the order "I feel as you do"—a kind of empathic support for what they felt and for this exercise of writing it out. But in this experimental period the shift of emphasis was bound to be inconsistently handled. There were trace elements of the previous postures still obtaining:

"Is the Remembrance Service Necessary?" (the student's assignment)

This is promising but your mechanics are rather careless [seven errors in two pages]. Never write in pencil again, no matter what the excuse [in pencil]. . . . Comment on my comments please. (Mr. Smith)

I think your comment was just. (student)

[A second book] . . . [it's] as though you had read my work. . . . I know I can try and correct my mistakes and do better the next time. (student)

I'm glad this impression comes over. (Mr. Smith, "Thought Books": 10A)

However, what also emerges from comments like these is something stronger than the proposed "connection between their own lives and what they read." It is an intimacy which can serve to forge a new link between the teacher and student. The strength of these connections has often been the therapist's problem, but it is just as much a part of how the talking cure works. In this case the therapeutic effect—of integration—is achieved as the student realizes this greater sense of self by connecting with the teacher through writing in a way not experienced before:

> "The Problems of Childhood" . . . . You could now say that I have finally found myself, if people accept me great, if not it's their loss. (the student's assignment)
>
> A charming and convincing piece of writing. I accept you—and am sorry for offending you. (Mr. Smith)
>
> Thank you very much I am glad you feel that way. I did have my doubts. . . . But I understand and I was at fault too. (student comment)
>
> You really are delightful. . . . (Mr. Smith, "Thought Books": 10A)

It is helpful to recall that the grade 10 academic "B" students were considered to provide the best starting point for this program. Though they are "academic" students, there is not the same opportunity for engagement in literature with these students. Yet while they were "tolerably well motivated to follow up a teacher's suggestions," they tended to be "less confident about using language as a whole" (Mr. Smith, January 11). Language for Learning holds out a means of drawing these in-between students into the subject, into a certain involvement in the English class. It is a way for the teacher to connect, rather than just leading the students up to work after work of literature. There is no distinguishing, on the one hand, the more active engagement in the class and with the teacher (as the trusted adult), against and, on the other, the acclaimed greater self-understanding and general "learning." This does not deny the possibilities of this movement and what it can realize in the students' writing. It does have the ability to connect. Rather, my comments are meant to bring to light what it is reluctant to admit.

There remains the question of Language for Learning and the general level student:

> The principles would be exactly the same for the general. I would say you just provide them more opportunities to write and to talk. . . . The generals, well what about them? Many of them don't have opportunities at home [to talk]. . . . But they do talk amongst themselves. What I would say is that they need to get used to talking about things. . . . In encouraging them to write and write and write, and to talk and talk and talk, under direction, then we can get them to use their language resources better. (Mr. Smith, February 15)

Mr. Allen seemed less sure of the resource situation; he had referred at the workshop to students with "very poor language resources . . . not using language to think" (January 25). He had taught general level courses up to last year. Mr. Russell and Ms. MacLeod, with their greater proximity to the program, were more decisive about the relationship of the general level student to the Language for Learning approach:

> Oh, I know it's a big thing in this school [but] **these** kids, they bomb out; they don't know where to begin to be creative. (Mr. Russell, December 8)

> Keeping a journal doesn't work . . . won't explore feelings . . . [it's] too abstract. (Ms. MacLeod, December 9)

> [After a further session of experimenting with it] I wanted them to write about their fears. . . . Were they like or unlike any of the characters. . . . The directions have to be so specific and they're very concerned about length. They're not into expressing their feelings, as I said before it's too abstract. . . . They'd rather do exercises. . . . I can't get them to do more than a paragraph. (Ms. MacLeod, February 15)

Ms. MacLeod had respected and enjoyed these students for their very ability to express their feelings honestly (December 9). How is it so changed in this case? The students were not as prepared to take their coats off as this approach so demands—to open themselves to an English class that wants more **of** them than just **from** them. They were perhaps not so ready to drop the instrumental approach—"how much for how many marks"—in exchange for self-improvement and a new more intimate rapport with the teacher. They are no longer as eager to turn to the school for a sense of belonging or intimacy. Still, Mr. Smith would surely claim that this writing is not "to abstract" and he would be right; but in its explicitness it is too risky, too demanding. With writing the general students have little enough reason to believe they could hold their own, in the way some of them can orally in the classroom. Ms. MacLeod had not failed to recognize this oral strength. She took advantage of her small class to talk casually with them about movies, their neighborhood, the news and one day, their secret fears. Yet with regard to the willingness to write, there is a danger of taking too much from Ms. MacLeod's characterization of her class; the potential for writing was there to be found as well:

> "I like reading, but I like writing more. I can write for days and hours dealing with feelings and people" (10Gf:94).

However, this girl had less chance of influencing the teacher's response to the program for reasons to be discussed more fully on the question of gender distinctions in teaching general level English.

A serious consequence of this lesson learned by both of the general level teachers is that one of the very few opportunities to write outside of the overiding concern with conventions, which Language for Learning offers, is lost to these students. While it is difficult to know what difference this would make, the students, in the few opportunities they had with it, decided it would not be much against what it would ask in return:

> Some of you have trouble talking about yourselves. Part of the problem is deciding if you can trust me. . . . [To Jane] you were not quite on the topic. You were to adopt the role of social worker and write about yourself. One of the problems was to relax. . . .You probably asked yourself, "what is Russell looking for" [when I assigned topics like] "Who am I?". . . . "You be me" [take a teacher's perspective of self]. . . . A social worker is concerned about your social situation. Are you living at home? Do you have both parents? [Holds up an exemplary piece: it looks like an office form with categories filled in.] Some of you are asking, "why are you getting away from grammar" and "what is he up to?" I'm not interested in you. . . . I'm interested in your revealing yourself to you. To work out through the pen. I'm actually getting full pages—some even two. . . . I'll be honest, I wasn't sure where I was going with this. This is the ultimate writing [assignment]: a social worker's report [on yourselves]. . . . You should feel less threatened. . . . Ready for the next stage—to study poetry, to look at poetry from the personal point of view. . . . The opening poem in the text book, normally it doesn't work, but it will with us; I think it will. . . . [To Alex] take off your jacket and relax . . . (Mr. Russell, 12G, February 2)

Not quite beyond, but as part of what teachers have learned about teaching in the streams, are two other attitudes which seem to have been forged through the day-to-day managing of the English class. Prejudicial responses with regard to gender and race may well have been brought to the classroom, but once there they have been refined and made more specific, if only through their more open realization: "I wasn't prejudiced before coming to this school" (Mr. Russell, January 19).

I would begin with the simple observation that there is a kind of male dominance acknowledged by the teachers in the two general level classes. A corresponding inverse of that dominance—an extra female presence in the academic classes—was not realized, though if it were a matter of numbers alone it should have been. It is rather that with the academic class the extra attention is paid to the discipline of English. (In the one academic class where the degree of attention paid to the female students did seem to run beyond mere numbers, it was a matter of the teacher's sense of his own charm; the female students didn't dominate or have a greater influence by virtue of this attention, only the teacher did.)

In general level classes, interestingly enough, the starting point of this greater male influence was language. For example, the authority which the teachers would command by the sheer assertion of loudness—not shouting, but a firm clear room-filling quality—is openly met and challenged by a few of the male and somewhat fewer of the female students in the general classes. They have established, at least in the classroom, their right to be heard. Equally so, they've challenged the teachers's authority in allocating the right to speak. The teacher, in turn, has learned to recognize and respond to the extra-presence of these students. They are seen to hold the balance of power, as a factor of their willingness to co-operate. When the teacher reads the attitude of the class, responds to its mood or generalizes about it, you can sense it is a handful of these male students that are being spoken for: "I was going to do poetry today. I took one look and said no, not with these kids. . . . I handed out the texts instead" (Mr. Russell, 12G, January 13). The teacher becomes especially sensitive to incorporating these students, to bringing them along with the lesson:

> Did you see how I used that sucker [he pulls a lollipop out of his chest pocket to show me; he had thanked a "tough" student during the class for bringing it in for him]. I picked it from the breakfast table; I took it from my daughter. . . . They ["tough" students] need that. He does. . . . just some attention at the beginning and then he's O. K. . . . You've got to have these games and tricks to hold their interest. (Mr. Russell, November 16)

> He tries to pull that psychology on us—really strange! (student, 12G, November 18)

> Are these [the "black" Donnellys] the kind of people you's like to live beside David? ("I **do** live next door to people like that.") . . . Are you going to raise your kids that way David? ("Yup."). . . . (Ms. MacLeod, December 10)

But it goes beyond the extra attention that is paid to these students. The novels, for example, especially those Ms. MacLeod terms the "gang novels" (stories about male teenage gangs), are meant to meet the tastes of these "tough" male students. Though S. E. Hinton who wrote **The Outsiders** (1967) and **That Was Then, This Is Now** (1971), two of the prescribed "gang novels" for the general program, is Susan Hinton, she takes on in both a male persona to narrate the struggle and the stereotyping. To complement the urbanity of these and other books on the course in this genre (for example, **West Side Story**), there is Farley Mowat's portrayal of **man** against nature, **Two Against the North** (1977). **The Black Donnellys: The True Story of Canada's Most Barbaric Feud** (Kelly 1974) had been a special selection of Ms. MacLeod's and provided the literary focus during the second term for the general level grade tens. She had mentioned at the workshop on the general program that both she and the students had had enough of the "gang novels" (January 25).

When I inquired about the bulletin board display which had clippings on

Margaret Atwood and on rape prevention, Ms. MacLeod told me that Mr. Smith had asked for bulletin board displays; Atwood was for Canadian literature (Grade 11) and rape prevention was for the generals (December 18). She advised me that they had not been displayed, as I had suggested by my question, out of a feminist interest; it was, she indicated, a matter of appealing to the students' interests.

In the actual running of the class, Ms. MacLeod spent the first few minutes, before the boys made it in, chatting with the three or four female students in a quiet and friendly way. Once the boys did arrive, they began to absorb increasing amounts of attention either through their extreme expressions of withdrawal—head down or magazine reading—or by their taking it upon themselves to interject. There was, in both Ms. MacLeod's and Mr. Russell's classes, at least one female student who had an equal impact on the proceedings, yet in return these female students were open to an extra and sometimes unpleasant teasing from the dominant male students—"You look like Aunt Jemima now" (12G, February 10).

This recognition of a certain male dominance in the general classes by the teachers is matched by a similar sense in the students.[17] The female academic students felt there was no discrimination at Kipling and that what female students said was received fairly enough. The female general students also felt it was fair, yet they expressed sentiments, on occasion, which suggested that the class might do well to consider the question of sexism, instead of contributing further to it:

> Males, they sound like they know more. Ladies, like us, they basically just talk about home life. Like men, they go into education, like business or stuff like that. ("Think you'll have a fair chance in 'Accounting' then?") Oh yes. (12Gf:15)

> It's true [girls talk too much]. I do it myself. I talk gossip. Everybody does, and not bad gossip. (12Gf:05)

The significance of these gender distinctions leads indirectly back to the issue of standard English. To be well-spoken, as some of the students realize, is a source of strength and confidence:

> It would make me feel confident . . . if I said something and it came out well and powerful. (12Af:40)

> I would make an answer knowing that to my knowledge it is right. (12Gm:04)

It allows one to speak one's mind without feeling foolish, or "sounding dumb" in the students' terms; though it might also inhibit a response out of a concern with propriety. However, there is in the classroom another source of confidence and authority, another grounds for speaking up, both in volume and self-representation. This alternative, through sheer bravado in class is, then, mainly a male sport. It is a source of privilege that will not easily be denied to them; what is at stake for these male students is the threat of emasculation which compliance with the school can represent. The male students have a means of meeting this threat to their self-esteem which the female students do not as readily have as part of their normal repertoire of social roles. The rather loud and assertive actions of these students in the general level classroom undermines standard English, as an instrument of exclusion. It is, however, not allowed to go unchallenged:

> Sam had a good idea but he doesn't present it right. . . . He cut me off. He can't just jump in. I told him you can cut your family or your friends off but not here. He said O.K., next time he'd remember. (Mr. Russell, January 13)

> I noticed that in Russell's class that if you sort of blurt out he'll always put you down, like he notes that you did that. (12Gm:96)

It is of course not quite on a par with being well spoken—you do get "put down"—but it continues in the general level classes to provide a power of expression in the classroom which is fully met by the attentions of the teachers. It is not solely a male privilege, but this is very close to what it means in these classes.

Among the English teachers of Kipling, black students constitute something of a linguistic entity and not a very promising one:

> I've got two blacks. . . . Really lousy standard English . . . a dialect . . . no verb agreement. . . . But for "What I'd like to be," they wrote genuinely moving stuff. (Mr. Smith, November 9)

> There is one [problem] with endings; some have no concept of endings—"ed," "ing," "s"—they just leave them off . . . missing completely. ("Who does?") The black kids mainly. It is a dialectical problem. . . . They don't hear them [verb endings] and they don't see them really. (Mr. Alcott, Writing Centre, November 30)

> With substandard you can't communicate. . . . Most blacks are sensitive to this. I don't usually watch "The Jeffersons," but I did to jot down patterns [for English as a Second Language class]. Jefferson's supposedly in business; he should be using standard English. . . . He's too lazy, yet he has a responsibility to change. (Mr. Russell, December 8)[18]

In each of the conversations above I had asked if they would identify general language problems or areas needing work in the students' writing. In class there was a good deal of tolerance shown with the students' speech; Ms. MacLeod, for instance, had decided against correcting oral errors completely. However, in the written work the full weight of these linguistic differences was brought to bear:

Now it matter here; you supposed to be more grownup. You don't expect a baby to talk perfect English, do you? They [grade twelve students] should, it's the last year here. (12Gf:16)

They always look for the little stuff. You use past tense and present tense and grammar.... They'll lookout for grammar; when you get back the paper ... you see all kinds of mistakes.... By the way you speak they know you didn't do that good in school.... (12Gf:15)

However, this sensitivity to a "black dialect" must be considered along with the other racial attitudes the teachers had developed through their work. Both Ms. MacLeod and Mr. Russell made reference to how an active black community group could interfere with their handling of the students. Mr. Russell had tried to have a girl removed from his class for her sporadic attendance and surly tardiness. He had carefully documented his case, but because her father was on the executive of this black community group, he believes the school's administration backed down and would not support him (Mr. Russell, January 19). It was this anecdote that was prefaced by his statement: "I wasn't prejudiced before coming to this school."[19] Ms. MacLeod mentioned half-jokingly that she thought she might run into some trouble from this same group for having managed to have a second black student, Bob, removed from her general level grade ten class that year.[20] This had also been a response to an attendance cum attitude problem (Ms. MacLeod, December 9). It seems obvious enough that this community group has become a presence in the school. Rather than being responsible for creating prejudice, as Mr. Russell suggested, it seems to be working quite effectively at raising the question of prejudice where others would prefer not to admit it.

The question didn't emerge where it might have, however, in the literature lessons of the general level grade ten class. It was not just missing from the discussions of the book, **The Black Donnellys,** but in the inevitable test question on why they were called the **black** Donnellys. The answer was given in class by a black student who later told me that he'd only read the first four chapters of the book and picked up the rest in class, enough of it, at least, to do "well" on the test:

I got one! [one mark; he is asked to read his answer.] Because the Donnellys were a bad family and caused lots of damages and hurt lots of people.... Black as evil. (10Gm:93)

In place of a heart there was a blackness... because they were heartless and cruel. (Ms. MacLeod, in a teacher reiteration, January 10)

There was no discussion of implications of this association; in fact, the association was reinforced—the student got a mark for it. In discussing this point with Ms. MacLeod, she said to me that she thought her distinction—blackness in place of a heart—had kept it clear of racial overtones (February 15). The only incidents of black students complaining, she told me by way of explaining her lack of concern, were in academic classes where, for example, a girl had found the portrayal of blacks in **To Kill a Mockingbird** distasteful. The student had been given another book to read.

There are issues which so touch the lives of the students in this school that the teachers would hardly dare to touch on them in their teaching. It would only interfere, unnecessarily, in the students' learning of their true significance. To raise the consequences of being black, female or general at Kipling High School is to introduce into the discussion the school's authority to judge—to exclude and affirm—through, in this case of English teaching, language differences. It is to also draw near the sources of the teachers' prejudices which have become sharpened and focused in the service of this power. Thus, there is much in the area of language and society which is so close at hand, and yet quite beyond the goal of the department "to help students in their exploration of moral values" (**KHSCD** 82/83, p. 10).

4
Learning English
The Way the Queen Talks

21. What teachers don't really understand is—the anxiety that goes on in a silent student's life. (12Af:41)

32. Those who have a way with words—have away with everything. (10Gf:91)

40. You forgot—not all of us are as dumb as we think and act. (12Gm:10)

Knowing what has been intended and what has been taught in the English classrooms at Kipling provides only a vague indication of what has been learned by the students about their mother tongue. Though the school is our single-minded answer to the need we feel to teach these young minds, they, in turn, are not equally given to this kind of restriction in their learning. There are many lessons out of school. For this reason I have separated the chapters on teaching and learning, though not completely. Some of what is taught is learned. Yet I do not wish to hold the teachers responsible for all that is understood by these students. What can be stated, at the very least, is that the students hold the views I am about to describe in the face of the previously outlined teaching. With less certainty, though still with some measure of clarity, associations and continuities between teaching and learning can be pointed out. Finally, there are those interesting discontinuities to be considered—that is, a sense made of language in spite of what the teachers would teach. There was, at any rate, no absence of learning. Though, items were left blank on the Sentence Completion Test (SCT) which I employed to measure attitudes, in the conversations I had with students about language there were very few hesitations (Table 1). The students had learned their diverse lessons well enough; they had come to understand the significance of standard English.

The students' understanding and attitudes, however, proved to be often differentiated along certain dimensions. There are two primary groupings used in

Table 1   Sentence Completion Test Items

1. When I'm 25 I expect to be
2. I guess I'm
3. Reading
4. Standard English is
5. As an English student I'm considered
6. I read
7. Teachers talk
8. What makes me different is
9. One contradiction in this school is
10. Middle class talk is
11. All this schooling will
12. The ones who get treated badly here
13. Writing
14. Students in the general English classes
15. The message I get from this school is
16. Males talk
17. One of the main things I've learned about language here
18. It's no use to
19. Working class talk
20. The reason some students do well in English is
21. What teachers really don't understand is
22. Students in the academic English classes
23. Females talk
24. English classes here are concerned with
25. What we have in common in this class is
26. I am most careful about my language when
27. Literature
28. School does give you the chance to
29. People learn to speak standard English by
30. The reason teachers want us to use standard English is
31. Books
32. Those who have a way with words
33. The students here take seriously
34. If I did speak and write standard English
35. The staff here take seriously
36. The most important use of language in our society
37. I might make my feelings and ideas known more if
38. What has made my own life clearer to me
39. Language is used in this school to
40. You forgot

organizing young people in schools: by age and "academic aptitude." People are transformed into students along these two dimensions, but not only these two. Gender distinctions are also present, though not, of course, solely as a school creation. Gender lends a third dimension to school records but also, in this case, to how certain aspects of language are understood. In fact, it proved to be principally the dimensions of academic stream and gender which served to distinguish, in varying degrees and with different issues, the students' response to the Sentence Completion Test on language in the high school. That is, with all of the certainty the mathematics of probabilities and levels of confidence can provide, it would seem that the students' regard for language differs by academic level and gender.

I wish to begin this statistical examination with what is certainly the most general and yet positive assertion I can make—that is, whether an item received any response at all. The best any of the items did was to receive responses from all but three or four of the ninety-six students. Items which drew the greatest number of completions were some of the simplest: "3. Reading—" or "7. Teachers talk—" (both with a 93% response), though not "27, Literature—" (68%).

But then some of the more complex items did equally well, suggesting that for these items explanations are commonplace, if not essential, to the culture of the school: "20. The reasons students do well—" (97% response). The initial more personal items proved to be no guarantee: "2. I guess I'm— (83% response). Wherever and whatever the item, it had to touch on a concern which the students had faced up to previously: "11. All this schooling will—" (97%) and "28. School gives you a chance to—" (95%).

There was a significant difference (significant at the .05 level) between the greater tendency of academic students to respond in the case of 44% (17) of the forty items on the SCT.[1] On 18% (7) of the items, the number of female students who responded was significantly greater than the number of male students, and similarly with 10% (4) of the items for the grade twelve students compared to those in grade ten. The largest discrepancies were between the academic levels on the final ten items of the SCT, though not without exception. While item "31. Books—," for instance, elicited no significant differences in response level along any of the three variables, "30. The reason teachers want us to use standard English—," had the largest significant difference (significant at the .0001 level) between the different response levels of the two streams. It was not just a matter of unfamiliar terminology, as "4. Standard English—" had received a completion from 83% of the students. Rather than the term, it was the **reason** teachers were promoting standard English which did not engage the interest of the general level students. It suggests that many of them cared little or had not bought the reasons the other students, particularly the academic ones, were given to suggesting: that it is proper (28% of the students), understandable (18%) or common (12%). Yet one can go only so far with this lack of response; perhaps the strongest evidence I have against second guessing the meaning of these student decisions to skip over an item is in Edward's failure to complete item "27. Literature—." In the interview he proved to be the most articulate spokesperson literature could wish for, as can be seen from his comments used in the previous chapter.

I have decided not to include a statistical analysis of all forty items on the SCT in this study.[2] I have chosen to describe the results of four groups of items which bear directly on the students' understanding of language. The first set covers the students' response to literacy in general; the second to the specific issue of standard English; the third introduces the school's concern with language; and the fourth touches on language groups or labels in our society. In this statistical description I have attempted to provide a general picture of the pattern of responses within the entire student sample, while bringing to light the points at which there is a significant statistical difference along the variables of either level, gender or grade.

The first set provides an indication of differing attitudes towards language activities. The female students were significantly more positive in their responses to "3. Reading—" (Table 2). The historical precedence of this greater proclivity has been reviewed by Watt in his study of the rise of the novel (1973). He suggests that the "tendency for literature to become a primarily feminine pursuit" in the eighteenth centure was a result of an increase in leisure time (pp. 410-11).[3]

This item on reading was also one, of only two items, in which there was an equally significant positive response from the academic students. It suggests that these differences, in the case of reading, are as much a matter of gender as stream (Table 2). The general students did tend to be more conditional in their response: "Reading—is good if the material is good" (12Gm:10). Theirs would seem to be a slightly more critical acceptance of the activity. Academics, one would think, are as discerning in what they actually read and enjoy, but they have expressed, on occasion, a more unqualified adherence to the value of reading and books:

No matter how bad the book is you can always learn something from it. (Lisa, 12Af:38)

No matter what they are about you'll always learn something. (12Af:34)

I never thought of this before but its almost as if the book has sort of a higher position on the sort of pecking order of media. (Edward, 12Am:33)[4]

Table 2   **Item 3. Reading—**

(N=96)	General (53)	Academic (73)	Female (48)	Male (48)
No Response	13%	0%	0%	15%
Negative	13	5	6	13
Neutral	8	7	4	10
Positive	45	77 **	75	44 **
Conditional †	21	12	15	19
	100 ‡	100	100	100

† Conditional refers to statements such as "—is fun if the book is good."

‡ Due to rounding off some columns do not add up to 100.

** Significant at the .01 level.

Note: The category with a significant difference is found by re-partitioning the table (with a significant chi-square value) using a 2 x 2 table (positive, non-positive by general, academic), and recalculating the chi-square and level of significance with one degree of freedom. The same partitioning procedure used with other categories did not, in this case, produce significant chi-square values (Castellan 1965).

When the material is good or when the time is right, 66% of the general students consider reading favorably: "I always did like reading" (10Gf:88). The students in the general stream do show an encouraging response toward these activities, especially if regarded in light of what one is led to expect: "The difference is night and day.... These kids are marked by a lack of wanting to read" (Ms. MacLeod, December 9). It is equally encouraging in light of the fairly negative and certainly reluctant participation of a few who can often enough dominate the class: "Ask who liked it?" "It bored on too long!" (students on completing the assigned novel; 12G, January 5). There were only seven students (13%) at the general level who wrote negative comments for the item, "Reading—."

With the other item which touched explicitly on reading, "6. I read—," there were no significant differences between the streams or the sexes (Table 3). Reading and books do not seem to have become strongly associated with school, even on a questionnaire completed well within that very context. Though the item is somewhat leading, the high response rate (94%) and sense of personal involvement (rather than a mere description of titles) suggest a strong identification of reading

Table 3   Item 6. I read—

(N=96)	Grade 10 (44)	Grade 12 (52)
No Response	14%	0%
Denial	7	2
For School	14	10
For Self	66	89 **
	100	100

** Significant at the .01 level.

with the self, again where it is not assumed to flourish, at the general level:

6. I read—sad novels with more understanding to us teenagers. (10Gf:94)

—because I enjoy it. (12Gf:17)

—as much as possible where I can relax and enjoy my book. (12Gf:22)

These results, along with non-significant differences between the academic levels, need to be considered in combination with the low number of negative responses to "Reading—" by the general level students. This sense of literacy should be kept in mind, for instance, when considering the "bad experiences" with print which many of these students are assumed to have had—the frustration of learning to read, the denial of their lives in the books and the meaninglessness of many of the texts (Dennison 1969; Martell 1976; Bettleheim and Zelan 1982). These findings would suggest that the students have understood that the negative experiences arise out of the classroom rather than the book; students do drop out of classes, lash out at school staff or more often quietly accept their judgements—but they also come to think of themselves as readers. The general students are not, for example, as positive about English classes (see below, Table 15). The case with items "27. Literature—" and "31. Books—" was similar; there was a greater positive response by the academic students as a whole, but it was not in either case a statistically significant one (Table 4).

This rather affirmative approach to literacy on the part of the students tends to collapse with the response to "13. Writing—" (Table 5). There is a significant difference of attitude between the general and academic levels, both in connotation and sense of function. Though there is an overall drop in the number of positive

Table 4   Item 27. Literature—;   Item 31. Books—

| | Literature— | | Books— | |
| | General | Academic | General | Academic |
(N=96)	(53)	(43)	(53)	(43)
No Response	45%	19%	26%	14%
Negative	13	9	5	0
Neutral	11	21	17	12
Positive	23	40	38	54
Conditional	8	12	9	21
	100	100	100	100

responses to writing, as compared to reading, it is especially dramatic for the general level students. The number of positive comments, when compared to reading, drops by more than half and the number of negative ones more than doubles. The matter of standard English—as **the** point of evaluation—bears very heavily on this. Correction doesn't have to be viewed in a negative fashion, as one student neatly demonstrated: "13. Writing—in a class helps because if making mistakes they can be corrected immediately" (12Gf:20). But more often it is not so graciously received:

> I like to write, but I have very bad spelling and that frustrates me a lot. (Bob, 12Gm:19)

> Can't stand it. You make all kinds of mistakes. . . . They mark all my mistakes take my word for it. (12Af:16)

> —is very hard for me. I'm very sloppy and make mistakes. (12Gf:05)

"Sloppiness" is not irrelevant, especially at the general level; it is only one removed from Ms. MacLeod's ascription of "carelessness." It is something of the significance which writing has for this particular student after twelve years of schooling; it is the lesson she has learned on what the school and the world expect from a student, especially, perhaps, from a female student. The evaluation of writing begins to approximate more personal and encompassing judgements—in sloppiness and carelessness. Capabilities with standard English have been shown to have a minimal impact on academic success with reading (Troike 1970; Schwartz 1980), but they have been made crucial to writing. Even with the enriched academics, where standard English is no longer the issue, the discomfort still involved form: "It's the **strictness** of essays you can't do this and you can't do that" (12Af:34).

The general level students were also more likely to disassociate their response from the self, placing it more often in a school context:

13. Writing—is for the writers. (12Gm:21)

—nothing on a test. (12Gm:23)

—is hard and a real task. (12Gm:77)

—is too much work. (10Gf:90)

One manner of explaining this decline and disassociation with regard to the active aspect of literacy is to consider the kind of press the writing of the students has received. I do not mean "press" in the sociological sense of a pervasive influence, though such a use has some relevance in this case, but in a writer's sense. The reviews have not always been kind. There have, at least, been notices; but the critic consistently turns out to be the only audience. There is no public, no book sales or box office, to fall back on, to provide vindication, to prove how wrong the critic may have been. It is surely enough to make one wary, and rather weary of starting another piece, of opening another show.

Reading, on the other hand, is an experience protected from the careful scrutiny of the school. The ability to read is evaluated, but only indirectly and most often through writing.[5] Writing, on the other hand, becomes associated with fixed and demanding expectations which reading resists:

Writing is fun if you're in the mood for it. I hate writing for a deadline it makes me nervous. (10Af:53)

Essays are a problem for me unfortunately, because its a set way and you have to . . . . (12Af:34)

It is easy enough to believe that reading and books have a life of their own outside of school; writing would seem to have less of one. Writing is the hard work of literacy, and in the school it would seem to be done solely that the students might be judged. But still there were a few people from all four classes who were writing out of school and on their own—keeping journals, writing short stories, recording feelings, noting cars. It suggests a kind of literary sub-culture, without benefit of community or recognition. There was one noteable exception to this isolation. In the enriched class the sense of literacy was such that there could spring up an informal community of writers, if only around the promise of a literary magazine that never quite happened: "The people who are part of it get together once a week and look at what we've written, dissect it, cut it up. Because of that I write outside of class assignments, usually short stories" (Edward, 12Am:33). It is to provide reason enough to write—friends who are writing.

In Mr. Smith's class there have been writing assignments which were intended to be written outside of a regard for either convention or teacher. However paradoxical this may be, it had produced in some students very positive attitudes towards writing as a means of self-exploration and understanding:

> I like that because it makes you think what you're thinking about. . . . It makes you in touch with yourself, how you're feeling. . . . It's a chance to get a break from working all day in school just to think about yourself. (10Af:54)

Yet with his class as a whole, the response to the item on writing was not significantly more positive when compared to the academic "enriched" grade twelve class, where in the university-prep ambience there was none of this "expressive" writing (Table 5). It might, perhaps, be that we are not as grateful for insights into ourselves as we might imagine. A more likely explanation, however, is to be found between the teacher's aspirations for "writing to yourself" and what these reasonably successful students have learned about school: "20. The reason students do well is—because they can really understand what the teacher wants" (10Af:55)

Table 5　　**Item 13. Writing—**

(N=96)	General (53)	Academic (43)	Academic Grade 10 (21)	Grade 12 (22)
No Response	23%	7%	5%	9%
Negative	28	7 *	5	9
Neutral	19	14	24	5
Positive	23	58 ***	57	59
Conditional	8	14	10	18
	100	100	100	100

* Siginificant at the .05 level.

*** Significant at the .001 level.

In this case it is the very innovation, intented to reduce writing just for the teacher, which makes it apparent that "reading" the teacher is more than an acquired bad habit of the student. It is writing in the school:

> There's just some things he says he wants and I interpret it—what I think he wants—and not totally right. (10Af:56; in reference to "expressive" writing)

> I sit there for a while; I don't really know what he wants. (10Af:63)

> It's just when you're writing something you never know if the teacher is going to like it. (10Af:61)

What these students do "know" is that there can be no writing without a sense of audience, and that one might as well be realistic about who the audience of consequence really is. They could hardly have become academic "A" students without a sensitivity to this presence—"the 'A's will always get on" (Mr. Smith, January 10).

There were four items in the SCT which employed the term "standard English." The first of these on the form, "4. Standard English is—," was intended to gain a sense of the currency the term had among the students. There was quite a significant difference (significant at the .0001 level) in the degree to which academic level students, compared to general level students, responded with "propriety" in one form or another (Table 6). Only slightly less significant was the greater penchant for propriety in the responses of the female students (Table 6).[6] Some of these students told me later in the interviews that they had been guessing: "4. Standard English is—what you use everyday; what is usually found in books and dictionaries" (Lisa, 12Af:38). Nonetheless, their guesses centered most often on notions of propriety, exaggerated or otherwise:

> 4. Standard English is—what British upper class men and women speak at tea time. (12Am:35)

> —that English which is spoken by people who know the proper way to speak. (10Af:70)

> —the only form of English that should be used. (12Am:36)

What is perhaps most interesting in what has been learned about standard English is that it is quite explicitly the one Mr. Smith does not want them to have. I had originally designed the SCT using the expression "proper English," as one I believed the students would most easily recognize in terms of the language form which they were being taught. Mr. Smith had, in our first conversation over the phone, objected to my use of "proper" as threatening to undo exactly what he was

Table 6   Item 4. Standard English is—

(N=96)	General (53)	Academic (43)	Female (48)	Male (48)
No Response	26%	5% *	15%	19%
In School Terms	17	4	17	4
Self	23	9	11	23
Vocation	2	2	2	2
Propriety	15	54 ****	44	21
Commoness	11	14	8	17
Other	11	7	4	15
	100	100	100	100

* Significant at the .05 level

**** Significant at the .0001 level.

working toward in language attitudes (November 6). It was his only objection to the form, and he accepted my substitution of the word "standard." Later, after my research was well under way he referred to how useful my "faux pas" about "proper" English had proved to be:

> What you did then is you underlined the fact that I've got to do something about talking in accurate linguistic terms. Part of the policy will be **not** to talk about correct and incorrect, proper and improper. The departmental policy will be in the future, I hope, to talk about standard and nonstandard English. (Mr. Smith, February 15)

The fact is, however, that to begin using accurate linguistic terms is not going to change much; a majority of the academic students already understand "standard" to be a reference to propriety. The new term may serve to obscure this connotation, burying it in the science of language, but it will also further authorize the distinction. In Mr. Smith's class during the course of my observations the common point of reference was the language of Her Majesty: "4. Standard English is—as Mr. Smith puts it, 'Would the Queen say that?' " (10Af:68; two of his other students also made reference to the Queen in response to item 4).[7] One of his students, who seems to have paid particular attention to the **Kipling English Primer** (see above, chapter three), did give an "accurate linguistic" description, with an added twist of career awareness: "4. Standard English is—the English

spoken by the majority of educated people when speaking professionally"
(10Am:72).

But the fact remains that the response to standard English often drew on the
ethics of language distinctions:

> 4. Standard English is—good, when it's not used people sound ignorant.
> (12Af:42)
>
> Like when people put the apostrophe in the wrong place, that's pitiful. (Lisa,
> 12Af:38)

Among the general level students the most common responses were in more
personal terms, and only indirectly a comment on its propriety:

> 4. Standard English is—a good thing to know. (12Gm:10)
>
> —boring, I couldn't care less how to speak properly just as long as what I say
> gets across to the other person. (12Gm:96)
>
> —not that very exciting. (10Gm:79)

In response to item 34. "If I did speak and write standard English—," the
academic students were significantly more likely to respond in terms of their own
use of the form, rather than in terms of the school—"my teacher would be happy"
(12Gf:17)—or a vocation—"I believe I would get a job easier" (12Gm:29; Table 7).
For a number of students it was not a particularly engaging proposal. Only half the
general level students responded to the item, yet of those who did there were
twenty of the twenty-six who looked on the idea favorably (Table 8):

> 34. If I did speak and write standard English—I'd be smarter. (12Gf:12)

**Table 7   Item 34. If I did speak and
write standard English—**

(N=96)	General (53)	Academic (43)
No Response	49%	14% ***
In School Terms	23	19
Self	25	65 ***
Vocation	4	2
	100	100

*** Significant at the .001 level.

Table 8   **Item 34. If I did speak and write standard English—**

(N=96)	General (53)	Academic (43)
No Response	49%	14% **
Negative	8	21
Neutral	4	14
Positive	38	40 **
But I do	2	12
	100	100

** Siginificant at the .01 level.

—I'd be an "A" student because I'd be able to express myself. (Jane, 12Gf:16)

—I think I'd be a better person for it. (12Gf:28)

What must not be overlooked in these responses is the recognition of the superior intellectual, expressive and moral qualities of standard English; they also contain, at least in part, an explanation for a failure to succeed. It is an explanation focused on language as the basis for a deep-seated inadequacy—an inability to think and express oneself. Not surprisingly this did not emerge in the same way from the academic level students. Consistent with their appreciation of standard English as a matter of propriety, they were more concerned with its very **lack** of expressiveness:

34. If I did speak and write standard English—I'd probably sound fuddy-duddy and strange. (12Af:48)

—nobody does, I'd be a living anachronism. (12Am:35)

—I wouldn't be using my own feelings and expressions. (10Af:70)

This pattern of responses to the literacy items is not a straightforward one. The general level students who responded to the possibility of having standard English saw it as both useful and profound. They had not been as positive in their definitions of standard English (Table 9). But in this instance of possibility ("If I did. . ."), their recognition of its virtues seems to run beyond utility. The academic students, on the other hand, seemed to believe less was at stake, as one might with manners which one had and were not much concerned with at this point. The

Table 9   Item 9. Standard English is—

(N=96)	General (53)	Academic (43)
No Response	26%	5%
Negative	17	5
Neutral	40	56
Positive	17	35
	100	100

academic level students appeared to put greater faith in the substance—books—rather than in the form. There was, however, another element in the response to item 34. Six students frankly questioned its very premise—"Don't I?" (12Am:32); "If I did?" (12Gm:13). These students—12% of the academic level—would seem to believe in their abilities strongly enough to challenge the item, rather than merely respond. Yet with the remainder of the academic level students it appears to be more a matter of it exceeding their desire—"I'd probably sound fuddy-duddy"—rather than their grasp. A necessary "anachronism," they would handle it in an instrumental fashion, as a kind of resource management: "It's fine if you can speak both ways; you can really speak a cool way to your friends but you have to be able to talk to teachers and people for jobs" (Lisa, 12Af:38).

It is not a question of intelligence, expression or ultimately a matter of the person at all in this instance. As the "standard" form is much more of a possibility for these students—Mr. Allen, for example believed they had the basics—it is realized to be of much less importance. Whatever special properties the general level students have ascribed to standard English, the academic level students seem more likely to see them not in the form, but in themselves.

In response to the question of how people acquire standard English, there was significantly more support for the efficacy of schools from the female students in a way that did not distinguish the academic levels (Table 10). This distinction is partly one of specificity. The more frequent comments referring to listening—"listening to and mimicking others" (10Am:58)—do not preclude the school's part; they are just a little vague about the context, as opposed to, for instance, "taking an English class" (12Af:11). There is not enough in the response, certainly, to begin to ascribe a greater faith in schooling to female students; they merely tended to be more exact and specific.

Table 10   Item 9. People learn standard English by—

(N=96)	Female (48)	Male (48)
No Response	10%	5%
Attitudes	4	6
Family	8	4
Listening/Reading	35	23
Practise	4	17
Socializing	6	4
Through School	31	13 *
Other	0	4
	100	100

* Significant at the .05 level.

The most popular response to the question of acquisition was in terms of exposure: "reading and listening to others who are well educated" (10Af:53). This seems particularly misconceived. It is true that in environments where one's first language will not work, just such exposure, with an opportunity to practice the new language, will do the trick, especially for young people (see, for example, Macnamara 1973).[8] But where one's language does work to get things done and to have oneself understood, as it does in these classrooms, exposure to another form will hardly suffice, except to facilitate a degree of mimicry. A most important factor in this matter of dialect acquisition is the social identity which becomes associated with a language form; to learn the new form entails a realignment of self with a new social group. It must be a social group to which one aspires, foreseeing a basis of acceptance.

The school's approach, however, has been to try to convince the students that "nonstandard" forms will **not** work, or at least will be insufficient. It has been, in effect, to challenge the valadity and the coherence of the student's identity, when the promise and possibility of creating a new one around standard English would seem to offer little, at this point, except a disassociation from what one had known and been. The school's challenge is, of course, an arbitrary attempt to establish a language environment where only the standard will work (which is quite different from being plunked down in a strangely-spoken land whether, for instance, Poland or the board room of the Bank of Canada).

The response to this item on how standard English is learned suggested that only a small number of students (12%) had a reasonably accurate sense of how it is people acquire standard English—through family and attitude. The majority of students, with their comments on schooling, practice, and exposure, are speaking more accurately to their sense of responsibility. They have all been schooled; they have heard and read daily in the standard form. They understand that they have had the chance to acquire this proper manner of speaking.

Yet even as they tend to acknowledge that they have had the opportunity, the students seem to have varying opinions on the significance of standard English. While there were indications in the responses to item 34 of the profound consequences of the form, there was also a nearly unanimous agreement (88%) that being careful about language was a matter of social impression management (Table 11). There was only an occasional concern for a quality such as lucidity: "26.

Table 11   Item 26. I am most careful about my language when—

(N=96)	General (53)	Academic (43)
No Response	11%	2%
Clarity	2	7
Social Impression	85	91
Other	2	7
	100	100

I am most careful about my language when—I'm in a useful argument with someone, arguing abstracts and practicals" (12Af:50). It was more often:

26. I am most careful about my language when—around richer people who think they're it. (10Gf:91)

—I am speaking to someone who has a high potential (university). (12Gf:15)

—talking to anyone of importance, my elders, anyone more educated than I am etc. (12Am:30)

What is equally noticeable in this regard for social impression is the note of deference—they mean to be careful in "addressing people of authority" (12Af:47). The students have learned that "care" in the use of language is primarily a matter of showing respect. They seem to appreciate the medium primarily as a social resource—for that job interview, not to sound dumb, not to lose face. Though the thrust of the enriched and advanced academic classes has been on the "argument" of literature, these students do not appear to have gained a particularly strong aesthetic or intellectual sense of the langauge. The standard is a matter of propriety, and care for its use a question of difference. It is none the less so for the general students, with the important exception of those who expressed a sense of standard English as the threshold for expression and intelligence. They believe in the impression they make; they seem compelled to take this business of social impression and deference far too seriously. Yet it seems more than anyone would dare to disabuse them of; for example, Mr. Smith does not appear to intend as much

Table 12   Item 17. One of the main things I've learned about language here—

(N=74) †	Language Properties (28)	Personal Use (46)
Negative	14%	47%
Neutral	79	33
Positive	7	20
	100	100

† Number of missing responses: 22.

with his new policy of linguistic accuracy.

Further to this question of personal usage is "17. One of the main things I've learned about language here—" (Table 12). There were not significant differences along the three variables of level, gender or grade with this item. Of those who were disposed to respond, 63% felt the main thing had been in regard to their own use, and of those 47% felt the lesson had been one on their personal inadequacy: "17. One of the main things I've learned about language here—you are ignorant for not learning proper English" (12Gf:08).

It would seem that language is too close to the self for many of the students to be dealt with otherwise; it cannot be as it might with evaluation in Chemistry or Geometry—at worst a reflection on one's ability to learn. Evaluation in English is bound to say more than that, as are notions of correctness, sloppiness or careless-ness when applied to one's use of language. Yet if English cannot be as remote and impersonal as Geometry, must it reflect so badly on the language which students bring to school? It is this question which begins to raise a serious challenge to Mr. Smith's proposed new departmental policy: to begin speaking in accurate linguis-tic terms. As one needs a reason to believe, one needs even more of a reason to be taught. The students who have learned the form best—at the academic level—believe standard English is proper. This is the relevance of the subject—they recognize it as the prestige form of the language. Accurate linguistic terms, as I mentioned, could well be used to obscure the issue of prestige and denigrated forms. Mr. Smith, in his policy decision to drop the labels of "correct" and "incor-rect," is attempting to absolve the school of participation in matters of status and exclusion, as if to create a sanctuary from the reach of this power. A sheltered language workshop might allow for more experimentation and participation with-out fear of censure. But is it linguistically accurate to consider these language forms outside of their social context and significance?

There are two related ways of addressing this question. The first is to be found in the number of black parents who have rejected the sheltering, if not patronizing, use of vernacular reading texts with their children (Schwartz 1980). They would not have the school protect their children from the demands and reality of the society at large. This leads directly into the second issue, which is that whatever the policy, the school cannot withdraw from the social context of language forms. The staff and students have no other basis for understanding their language than by the response it receives in our society. Rather than attempting to establish an alternative basis for distinctions in a neutral regard for all dialects—itself quite impossible except in a limited and artificial manner—it would seem more realistic to thoroughly examine the distinctions in the students, the staff and the society. This would naturally raise questions of prejudice and discrimination; if pursued with rigor, it would not likely absolve the school's part in this process. That is to say, this course would certainly tend to be uncomfortable and possibly lethal for the order and authority of educational discourse. It is, nonetheless, exactly what the situation would require if we are to place language judgements and the reasons to learn new forms in their proper context—that is, to speak in accurate and precise terms about language in our society.

A final item on this matter of personal use is "37. I might make my feelings and ideas known more if—" (Table 13). The students' sense of their own inadequacy as speakers and writers accounted for 23% of the remarks : "—if I were more fluent in the English language (12Am:36); "—I just could express them right" (10Gm:87). This was not the most popular response, but it did range across the grades and academic levels and it does again bring into focus those sentiments felt by the students of not being able to express themselves in their mother tongue. One might regard this as too much of a linguistic absurdity, but apparently it can be taught, or at least, it can be learned. More students did feel that the inhibiting fact was their own attitude: "37. I might make my feelings and ideas known more if—I didn't think it would embarrass me" (10Af:63). The academic level students, however, were significantly more inclined to suggest that another forum, a change of environment, would make the difference. The possibility for greater self-expression seemed only to await opportunity:

> 37. I might make my feelings and ideas known more if—I wrote them and published them in the media. Voiced myself more. (12Af:40)
>
> —I had a loudspeaker. (12Am:51)

When asked to consider the focus of the English classes, the most frequent response (31%) accurately reflected the major concern of English classes with "literature"—reading and books (Table 14): "24. English classes here are con-

Table 13   Item 37. I might make my feelings known more if—

(N=96)	General (53)	Academic (43)
No Response	34%	2% ***
Other's Attitudes	4	19
Another Forum	8	26 *
Better Language	21	26
Changed Attitude	32	23
Other	2	5
	100	100

* Significant at the .05 level.

*** Significant at the .001 level.

Table 14   **Item 24. English classes here are concerned with—**

(N=96)	General (53)	Academic (43)
No Response	26%	5% *
Grades	2	19
Writing	6	16
Grammar	28	12
Reading and Books	25	40
All of Above	13	14
Other	0	14
	100	100

* Significant at the .05 level.

cerned with—forcing an appreciation of literature" (12Am:35). But not far behind the force of literature were a series of responses that touched on the traditional concerns of grammar:

—mostly your grammar and your letter writing. (12Gf:28)

—proper expression. (10Af:63)

—English grammatically and as thought. (12Am:51)

Mr. Allen's reaction to the number of responses (21%) suggested that grammar is still the concern of English classes had been a straightforward, though somewhat uncharacteristic, "Bullshit!" (December 10). He then shrugged it off as something Mr. Russell was still up to with the general level—an anachronism. However, it was students of both levels who did perceive it as a concern, if only in the broader sense of proper form; there were no significant differences on the point. The students seem to realize that even without grammar lessons or a grammar text, there can still be a concern with the formalities of language which pervades the class. Most of the students (64%) were rather neutral and simply descriptive about the English classes: "reading, writing, literature" (10Am:74; Table 15). The academic level students were, however, significantly more positive about the classes in their comments. The thrust of the positive and not-too-positive responses of the academic level students reflects the distinction in the approach to teaching which I

Table 15   Item 24. English classes here are concerned with—

(N=96)	General (53)	Academic (43)
No Response	26%	5% *
Negative	6	5
Neutral	64	63
Positive	4	28 **
	100	100

* Significant at the .05 level.

** Significant at the .01 level.

noted in the last chapter:

> 24. English classes here are concerned with—the expansion of the mind (mine is). (10Am:72)
>
> —satire, also trying to squeeze the meaning out of everything said into something vital. (12Af:43)
>
> —ideas more than grammar. (12Af:39)

The distinction is between the "expansion of the mind" and "mostly grammar," which matches, and, I believe, reinforces the general level students' sense of linguistic inadequacy. The actual study of grammar has been proven to do little in improving students' ability to express themselves. One can imagine, however, that a study of it could do a great deal to suggest that one's powers of expression are inadequate. As the focus of expression is on the level of the grammatical, what is in danger of being lost is much of the reason **for** expression in the general level classroom.

The case with the academic students is not quite a parallel one. Whereas they have been encouraged to realize the intellectual rigors of language, the academic students still tend to associate care in expression with notions of propriety and grammar. It can best be explained in terms of a social perceptiveness; they recognize what will count, which determines for them the significance of standard English.

There were five items which drew on a characterization of different language users—teachers, males, females, middle and working class. The first point of interest in the response of the students was the readiness to generalize, a readiness which suggested the prevalence of certain attitudes. For instance, "7. Teachers talk—" received the greatest number of responses, while "19. Working class talk—" received the least, at something less than 50% from the general level students. More male students responded to "23. Females talk—" than to "16. Males talk—," reflecting, one would think, a greater tendency in our society to distinguish females against the male norm. Males do not tend to constitute a separate linguistic group, at least in their own eyes, and to a lesser degree in the eyes of the female students as well (Table 16).

The responses to "Males talk—" actually produced one of the highest chi-square values when analysed by gender. There were few positive things said about male talk; when it was distinguished from the norm it was not to speak of its virtues:

> 16. Males talk—to make themselves sound like they never could get hurt. (12Gf:09)
>
> —about bullshit. (12Gf:04)

Female students were decidedly more negative (significant at the .001 level) about male talk while the male students tended towards the neutral ("—about girls and girls" 12Gm:29) which again is to affirm the adherence of male talk to the norm in their eyes.

Table 16   Item 16. Males talk—; Item 23. Females talk—

	Males talk		Females talk	
	Female	Male	Female	Male
(N=96)	(48)	(48)	(48)	(48)
No Response	21%	38%	17%	27%
Negative	50	10 ***	33	29
Neutral	25	50 *	40	35
Positive	4	2	10	8
	100	100	100	100

* Significant at the .05 level.

*** Significant at the .001 level.

This becomes more revealing when the response to "23. Females talk—" is introduced into the discussion. There was no disagreement between the genders on the distribution of responses to this item. There were seven more responses to item 23, and though there is a slightly greater number of positive comments, the real contrast with item 16 is the degree of agreement on the negative qualities of female talk—one third of both the male and female students saw little virtue in it:

> 23. Females talk—a lot about things such as make-up, fashions, etc. It gets boring. (10Af:67)
>
> —too much. (10Gm:75)

The lesser regard for male talk expressed by the female students suggests a resistance to their own denigration, yet it is a resistance which in many instances does not translate back into a support for the talk of females. That is, while female students broke with males to condemn "male talk," they participated equally in the disparagement of their own speech. In the preceding chapter on teaching English, I discussed how in the general level classes there was a greater effectiveness of male speech accepted by both students and teachers. It is also reflected in the responses to these two items.[9]

As it turns out the female students of the general stream were only slightly more negative, though not to a statistically significant degree, about their own talk (Table 17). The school's part in this, as I have suggested, is marked by both a compliance in its actions—teacher acknowledgement of the male's stronger voice in the running of the general level class—and a failure to broach the subject in the twelve years of "language study."[10] But there is a further element, as well, in the

Table 17   **Item 23. Females talk—**

| | Female Students | | Male Students | |
| | General | Academic | General | Academic |
(N=96)	(18)	(30)	(35)	(13)
No Response	17%	17%	31%	15%
Negative	44	27	29	31
Neutral	33	43	37	31
Positive	6	13	3	23
	100	100	100	100

fewer negative responses of the female academic students. The academic English class makes its contribution, however slight, to this difference in attitudes by virtue of the fact that attitudes and judgements do get discussed in the academic classes; the students have more reason to believe that there is a taking issue with these matters: "23. Females talk—with too many apprehensions, not enough aggression, confidence, and direction" (12Af:50).

However, there is reason why this should prove to be little more than a slight influence, if at all. The humanizing effect of the liberal education would appear to be somewhat restricted in scope in this regard. The male academic students, for example, were not any less negative than general level males on the issue of female talk (Table 17). Equally so, academic students as a whole were significantly more negative than general level students on working class talk (Table 18). What cannot be supported, at least from the reflection of attitudes on this SCT, is that there is a broadening effect, with regard to tolerance and open-mindedness, engendered by the intensive study of great literature.[11] It is perhaps a matter of useful and not-so-useful prejudices. The female academic students could surely do without a denigration of their talk and have, to a limited degree, thrown it off. What is at stake for the male academic students in item 23, however, is the ability to define yourself against what you understand to be female: "Females talk—in a somewhat simple and childish manner" (12Am:49). It is more than some of them are prepared to forego. Though there is certainly greater opportunity for insight into prejudice within the forum of the advanced classes, there is little effort made to

Table 18   **Item 19. Working class talk—; Item 10. Middle class talk—**

| | Working Class | | Middle Class | |
| | General | Academic | General | Academic |
(N=96)	(18)	(30)	(35)	(13)
No Response	51%	26% *	42%	16% *
Negative	11	30 *	21	21
Neutral	25	28	25	42
Positive	8	0	13	23
Conditional	6	0	0	0
	100	100	100	100

* Significant at the .05 level.

directly challenge dominant language attitudes. Thus the issue, as it were, does not come to mind for the male students, except perhaps with tongue in cheek: "23. Females talk—about dresses, boys, and gossip and complain how everyone else is sexist" (12Af:35).

The two items on social class were intended to raise with the students an issue which has concerned sociologists of language and education for the past two decades. Differences between middle and working class talk have been documented (Bernstein 1971) and they have been challenged (Rosen 1972); they have at least a great currency among educational theorists, including those working in Canada (Edwards 1979). I wished to test the sense these labels had for the subjects of these theories. Could it be said to be an issue at all with them? I would further set the stage for the students' rather unspectacular response by mentioning that it certainly proved to be an issue with Mr. Allen. He strenuously objected to my use of "working class" on the SCT, in a similar fashion to Mr. Smith's objection to "proper." He felt it was misleading to use the term, "working class":

> There just aren't any of those nice clear distinctions anymore. They're fully assimilated into a middle class which sort of lumps people together. There is a West End and its poor and—there are very strong distinctions about how they view themselves, about what they think are their possibilities, about what they think are the attitudes of authority . . . for example, they don't vote in elections. It's just not working class. . . . That's implanting a concept of working class—"O well John, he is my friend but he is working class." (Mr. Allen, December 8)

He was concerned that the exposure to my SCT form would legitimate a "false" distinction in the students' minds. He considered "poor" or "lower," however, acceptable. I found the diligence of his concern for protecting his students from an admittedly less-than-clear concept as remarkable as his sense of their susceptibility. It is, of course, very difficult to estimate the effect of my use of the term on the students. As it was with Mr. Smith's "proper," however, many of the students appeared not to be in a position to be **led** into these attitudes—a good number of them (60%) were already there (Table 18):

> 19. Working class talk—is more slang and bad English than middle class or standard English. (10Am:66)
>
> —about boring things, their wives gossip too. (10Af:55)
>
> —is common unstandard slangish. (10Am:57)

The academic level students, as I mentioned, were significantly more ill-disposed towards the language of the "working class." This may be, as with the male response to "female talk," a matter of self-definition by exclusion. Seven students responded to the item in terms of "work **in** class" (in a strictly school sense): "—is the best way to communicate without having the teacher yell" (10Af:52). The misconception speaks to the unfamiliarity of the term "working class" for some students (though, one could say that they, at least, were not mislead by my use of the term).

The item on middle class talk did not distinguish the two streams, except in response levels (Table 18). However, a few of the students in the general level twelve did use the two items to distinguish themselves:

> 10. Middle class talk—is where I am at.
> 19. Working class talk—consists of four letter swearing words. (12Gm:04)

> —is the language I understand.
> —is the talk spoke at home. (12Gf:02)

> —is my level of talk.
> —is no different from any other. (12Gm:10)

The enriched twelves appeared to have a finer sense of class distinctions; in many instances they found middle class talk as somewhat substandard, or at least they had it in contempt:

> 10. Middle class talk—is too much slang. (12Af:31)

> —is good for that class, but should not be mixed with correct standard English. (12Af:36)

> —is what two chartered accountants speak at lunch time. (12Af:35)

There were also indications in the response to other items that an awareness of class was not solely of my manufacture, though to be fair there was but one independent mention of "working class":

> 14. Students in the general English classes—are the working class who will leave school this year and will be out after a trade next year. (12Am:21)

> 15. The message I get from this school—is that everything works in a "class system." (12Af:40)

> 33. The students here take seriously the dispute between upper and lower class. (12Gf:09)

The distinctions are there; in the two items on class talk it hinged most often on questions of propriety in language. This was, for example, the basis of the negative comments by the academic students in their response to middle class talk, as it had been for their lack of interest in the possibility of speaking and writing standard English (item 34). In fact the profound sense of emptiness in middle class talk, expressed by two students, bears citing in contrast to their response to working class talks:

> 10. Middle class talk—is unreal, all abstracts, no reality to base views on. We have the silver spoon in our mouth. (12Af:50; "Working class talk—is something I wish I heard more of.")

> —of the daily routines and their feeling of being lost in a crowd. (12Af:44, "—of their hard days at work and their rotten pay.")

There is not enough in this to say exactly how the students are drawing on conceptions of class and language in our society to define themselves. The distinctions are, however, present for many of the students. Just as one of the main lessons learned about language at Kipling concerned their own inadequacies (item 17), it would seem possible that their knowledge of social distinctions will come to be understood in terms of their own language and their own situation.

Of course, Mr. Allen is still right; the distinctions are no longer as clear (though this is still not a comment on their viability). The students have, however, turned to more concrete social divisions to find themselves, and a number of them have tried to deny what they have found. The students did take the school's stream designation and its reputation quite seriously. The responses to the item on students in the general level clases elicited a strongly defensive reaction from both general and academic level students (Table 19):

Table 19   Item 14. Students in the general level class—

Item 22. Students in the academic level class—

| | General Students | | Academic Students | |
| | General | Academic | Female | Male |
(N=96)	(53)	(43)	(48)	(48)
No Response	21%	14%	15%	23%
Negative	26	30	2	8
Neutral	13	33 *	25	42
Positive	15	5	58	27 **
Defensive	25	19	0	0
	100	100	100	100

* Significant at the .05 level.

** Significant at the .01 level.

14. Students in the general English classes—are no dumber than the others, its just you can't understand as fast. (10Gf:87)

—are not as stupid as many believe them to be. (12Am:36)

—are not dumb just lazy. (12Gf:01)

What these defensive responses (22%), along with the clearly negative ones (28%), admit to is an image that the general level student has to live with or somehow deny. Streaming is part of the school' contribution to these formative years, where definitions, designations and explanations must be sought out to make something of oneself. Streaming serves in this process of self-definition, if only by providing a contrast: "Students in the general English classes—are not as bright or fortunate as some other students" (12Af:41).

Just as there were no significant differences between levels in responding to the item on students in the general level classes, there was a similar agreement in the response to students at the academic level. The significant difference which did emerge was between the genders. The female students were significantly more positive about students at the academic level (Table 19). The male students were not overly critical—in responding to snobbishness or braininess—they were simply inclined toward neutral responses and less willing to grant what others felt compelled to acknowledge:

22. Students in academic English classes—must be very smart. (10Af:89)

—are smarter. (12Gf:02)

—are a bunch of smart people who try to impress their teachers with fancy work. (12Gm:18)

That they **are** a bunch of smart people is not about to be challenged by the students; at worst, they add to this notion a kind of distaste: "—are planning to stay in school the rest of their lives" (12Gm:21). The positive comments tended to turn classroom practices at the academic level into virtues: "—like to have group discussions and arguments more than the general classes" (12Af:44); "—have good arguments" (12Af:40). There were, finally, references to the superior attitudes which served to distinguish the academics in a moral sense:

22. Students in the academic level classes—know where they want to go after the school year. (12Gf:20)

—are students working hard so they can go to college. (12Gf:07)

—want to be articulate and succeed in life. (12Am:37)

No single profile of student understanding and attitudes emerges from this analysis of the Sentence Completion Test. The students have indicated a great range of lessons learned on standard English and literacy. In the next chapter I hope to flesh out the statistics reported here with a detailed look at the comments of eight students on their individual educations in language. There are, however, a few distinctions I wish to draw from the work in this chapter: Where a grasp of standard English is not crucial, for instance in reading, literacy seems to be well enough received; where standard English is the point of evaluation and the measure of competence, as in writing, there is more than a decline in enthusiasm—literacy becomes little more than schooling. As with the literature program, reviewed in the preceding chapter, language loses—to the story with literature and to form and mechanics with writing. This matter of adherence to form is, of course, the point of entry into our language for the concept of standard English.

The significance for both the female and academic students rests largely in this concept of propriety. However archaic and empty it may seem to them on occasion, it is still regarded as the necessary and useful means of making one's way. Literature's labour's lost, I'm afraid, and the students have come to regard care with language as a matter of deference and politeness. But the history of the concept amounts to as much: "would the Queen say that?" is to ask "would I say it in her presence?" ("I often wonder if she swears—not that it really matters" 10Af:53). The standard has been prescribed and constructed over the last three hundred years in the name of refinement and polite learning. The prestige form was meant to distinguish, from the opening conversational gambit, the manner of person with whom one was faced. When expressed in these terms it does seem an archaic social custom; it proved to be, however, the lesson the honor students of the English language at Kipling High School have learned.

The significance of standard English for the general level student is less easy to treat so lightly, though it is as much the result of the historical intentions of the form. Some of these students have come to realize—in considering what their failure to measure up to the standard might mean—that there are intellectual, expressive and moral qualities which they are without, as they are without their form. The prestige form of the language could not be elevated higher; it could, after all, hardly mean more than being able to express oneself, being smart or being good. The fact is that some of these general level students cannot imagine it meaning less. Standard English must involve intellectual, expressive and moral qualities in order to justify its part in the judgements they sense others make about them, in the understanding they have gained of themselves and their language.

The lessons more equally shared by the students concern how personal inadequacy with language is often the issue in a literate society—to be fluent in one's mother tongue. Illich (1979) has brought under historical scrutiny the very necessity of a standard as a requirement for increased literacy. He reminds us that there was a time in Europe, quite forgotten, when reading and writing flourished without the benefit of standardized vernaculars. We have moved well beyond this point and, as some of these students demonstrated, we now believe there may not even be expression or understanding, let alone literacy, outside of the standard form. Of course, it is not a standard which can threaten to strike people dumb. That is a question of a power which can establish and fix the position of the prestige form. The school contributes by providing the reasons and the rationale for standard English. It instills as common sense that affirmation and exclusion by the language distinctions of academic level and gender are both the natural and necessary way of organizing life in a high school and a society. The political significance of standard English is, I am suggesting, in its service to this hegemony; the universality and superior qualities with which Standard English has been invested have made it seem essential for the ordering of language and discourse. Finally, I would add that this matter of power and dominance is not one of a secret conspiracy, but of struggle and assertion. At Kipling, on this issue of language, one can participate in the process with as little as a "peeve," a "click" and a "grasp":

> My biggest peeve in English is when people say "I did good" and I turn around
> and say "I did **well**!" It clicks with me. I'm always correcting people's English, so
> I think I have a fair grasp on what I'm talking about. (Bob, 12Gm:19)

5

The Significance of Standard English
Eight Students

Maybe later on when your're in college and you've made your way in the
world you won't care as much, but in high school I think you do care.
(Annie)

School is just pure theory. You can take the theory or you can make up
you own. (Chris)

The door's open. All you've got to do is...[laughter]. (Jane)

A statistical description, whatever its measures of certainty, falls short of
providing a sensitive and complete picture of what language has come to mean to
individual students. I intend in this chapter to draw on the comments of eight
students in order to illustrate individual positions and responses to the issues
raised in the two preceding chapters. Though I have chosen the different students
because of certain features in their positions—Ralph for his class sense of language and Lisa for her faith in books—they are not to be taken as types. They
represent, rather, individual ways of handling and integrating the significance
made of language differences in our society. The preceding chapters on the
intentions and practices of teaching, as well as the statistical profile of student
attitudes, should serve as a context in which to consider the sense these eight
students have made of language. I believe they capture the full range and effect of
standard English at Kipling High School.

I would not, however, distort the perspective these students might provide.
Ralph was a general level grade ten student. He was the only student of the twenty
interviewed who described his language in terms of social class:

Well, most of them ["upper class"] won't understand my language, some
language, that lower class use. (Ralph, 10Gm:93)

By "upper class," Ralph said he was referring to "big businessmen," while the staff of the school is, in his terms, "middle class," as well as much more tolerant and understanding. He stated that the teachers did not correct his speech in class, though with his written work, "they would correct it." There remained, however, a problem with the way Ralph spoke in class. On his SCT he mentioned that he talked too loudly and was "noisier thatn a lot of people." This sense he had of his language was not tied to the context of classroom demands for discipline and quiet, but was left in generalized terms, as simply the way he spoke: "5. As an English student I'm considered—an average student but talk too loud."[5]

It was, of course, not just a matter of volume, for when I inquired further it proved to be more specifically "I fool around but it's the right times . . . not stuff that would get her [Ms. MacLeod] mad." In a lesson on the run-on sentence, for example, Dale and he sang a snappy little jingle on "conjunctions" which he told me later was from the "Saturday cartoons." Ms. MacLeod didn't seem to take exception to this spontaneous contribution to the lesson (January 12). But Ralph is right, his manner is louder than many of the other students. The black students in the school don't hush it up, but display a noticeable oral strength in the corridors and classrooms. They are recognized as a linguistic subgroup; there was, I found in my interviews with the teachers, a readiness on the teachers' part to distinguish the black students with regard to dialect and surliness. Ralph seemed to have taken this sense of linguistic deviance and made it into "loudness." Though volume may seem a strange focus, it is a means for him of decriminalizing his language—as opposed to calling it "rudeness," for instance—while admitting the point of its intrusiveness as well taken. Were this all Ralph had learned about his language it might seem a slight lesson. But though it was believed to be loud, it was not considered to be clear:

> Most of the time if I just talk like lower class, something like that, then what I'm saying, it don't seem to come out like, it doesn't make sense, really. ("For you?") For me.

In this are the full consequences of "lower class" talk: a sense of linguistic inadequacy and a self-denial of fluency in one's mother tongue. If it was only for my benefit—I'm afraid I can barely believe that he meant it—he has recognized and is still participating in the most denigrating of racial stereotypes. These notions of loudness and not making sense were stated by Ralph in an unqualified and absolute sense; the original context of the classroom has been allowed to drop while the labels were retained. It may well be the school's way to treat its demands as if they were context-independent and thoroughly natural demands—"there needs to be order so you must put up your hands before talking." But the consequence of this, for the issue of standard English, is not so much to render anyone speechless—though it might do that as well—but is to have students believe themselves unintelligible in their speech.

Many of the students in the study have developed a defensive response to the labels of streaming. They drew on current explanations which seem less degrading than what they feared others believed: "14. Students in the general English classes—are not dumber than the others, its just you can't understand as fast."[1] There do not, however, seem to be such exonerating explanations as readily available for the sense of linguistic deficiency. There is no shortage of explanations, though, which speak plainly and simply to debility. Ralph touched on a number of them, as if they might be the common way of making sense of language in the school:

> 30. The reason teachers want us to use standard English is because—they want to understand us.

> 37. I might make my feelings and ideas known more if—I speak clearly.

Ralph handled the differences between academic levels strictly in school terms ("14. Students in the general English classes—are ones who will not go to college") which is basically how the school's course description booklet, for instance, handles it. He understands his language, however, as both class-bound and as decidedly inferior to the point of linguistic absurdity.[2] He accepts and carries with him the "fact" than he is too loud, which is to say irreverent and inopportune in his timing, and that he is inarticulate, even in addressing himself. The volume of his voice is actually quite comparable to the room-filling quality of a teacher's, and that is perhaps part of its fault. But it serves to render what he says quite distinctly; his loudness would seem, in fact, to be a kind of resistance, an attempt to challenge and to break through this (racial) sound barrier. The efforts of the teacher—"the teacher keeps telling me to quieten down"—are a part of the school's official response to his speech. As the remarks in the final section of Chapter Three indicate. The teachers understand it as distinctly black and a problem, if not wrong. Ralph's explanation of his deficiency by virtue of class rather than race is to accept the school's denial of its racial bigotry. It was Ralph, after all, who got one mark for his explanation of why the murderous Donnellys were called "black."

Jane, in the general level grade twelve class, was another black student who indicated she had learned of the deep inadequacy of her own language. Language was also, in fact, a point of real strength in her position within the class. She was the one female student in Mr. Russell's grade twelve English class who spoke when she would, on things as she saw them. Yet against this show of strength she had learned another lesson. She explained the process this way:

> I want to get a point across, it's very hard. I'm getting tied—tongue mixed-up. I give up in English [class]. I know what it is but I can't explain it properly; I don't bother with it. I want to get the point across, not be babbling about something else. I don't talk the answers, I speak something real sassy. (Jane, 12Gf:16)

And sass she does, with great facility. It is as if this is the only articulate role left open to her; it is the only presence she can have in the class and "not be babbling." Yet it clearly is not her first choice: "I want to get a point across." It is, however, all that her language, as she understands is, will allow her:

> 34. If I did speak and write standard English—I'd be an "A" student because I would be able to express myself.

> 37. I might make my feelings and ideas known more if—I could speak perfect English.

What begins to emerge from these remarks is a sense that standard English acts as a threshold requirement, not only for "A" studentdom, but for self-expression. Of course, Jane does, in the face of this understanding, express herself with great aplomb, and quite as freely, if not somewhat beyond, as the classroom would permit. Yet it is as if her sass and Ralph's loudness have been effectively denied the power of expression—reduced to a kind of white (black?) noise by the linguistic authority of standard and proper English in the classroom.

What makes this more poignant in Jane's case is the sense she has retained of her own capabilities, outside of this language issue:

> 2. I guess I'm—ambitious when it comes to dealing with my life and future.

> 8. What makes me different—is my ability to understand what is being said and done.

Yet this sense of drive and ability are almost more than she would allow herself to realize, except under the protective and defensive guise of humour.

> 5. As an English student I'm considered—smart. Hah, hah, what a laugh.

> The door is open all you've got to do is [laughter]. . . . Taken advantage of nothing, ain't got no time—I work; I had two of them [jobs] as a matter of fact.

I do not wish to imply that her English teacher, Mr. Russell, or any other of Jane's teachers, specifically intended these lessons for her; I did not see exactly where in the teaching these ideas might have been made plain. It is, rather, a part of their—Jane's and Mr. Russell's—shared understanding of the significance of language and racial differences. That these differences matter doesn't need to be taught to the students, it is a lesson that they can be trusted to learn on their own. The school's part in this is principally to allow the prejudice to go unchallenged, and to implicitly reinforce it through the official evaluation and informal judgements made in the English class. The result is, that for Ralph, Jane, and the other students, standard English becomes a limit to what they can make of themselves. For Jane, ultimately:"I can't get my point clear. My English isn't—like I say 'ain't'—it ain't perfect. . . . It [standard English] helps look more, how can I say, more respectable, more educated."

As I indicated, Ralph was the only student to explicitly describe his language in social class terms. But there was, much more frequently, another pervasive sense of class which was designated geographically by, as one student put it, the direction you turned on the way home from school.[3] This act revealed the students' place in the town, as either east enders—the "high class"—or west enders—not so.

9. One contradiction in this school is—you are considered an individual, but it is an East End School. West enders aren't treated equally. (Chris, 12Gm:25)

Though I want to deal with Chris' views on this matter, I wish to begin with Mary because she both openly admitted she was a west ender which was rare enough, and she was trying hard to turn the label around. Her efforts had, apparently, received some support from at least one teacher. She described the struggle as more of a psychological than an academic one:

Oh it's stupid. We shouldn't, like not because we're from the west end. We shouldn't put ourselves down. Some . . . say that people who stay out the east door [of the school] they're more high class than we west enders and when you find out you're in the same class you get better grades than they do, but they think just because they're from the east end and they thought they're better, they're richer, whatever. Comparing their education they ain't better than us; I never put myself down. . . . Our teacher was telling us never put ourselves down, between the west and east end, because basically we checked out the same. (Mary, 12Gf:15)

The teachers in the staffroom, including three of the teachers in this study, laughed, at the sheer lack of sophistication I suppose, when I told them of this encouragement Mary had received in one of her classes (February 15). In this matter, discretion was to be the better part of valor; these issues were hardly to be raised in the classroom. There had been, Mr. Allen had reassured me, a play put on by the students and staff in the previous year which had in humourous sketches characterized the students who hung around the "east end" and "west end" doors of the school. However, this dramatic catharsis had, it would seem, failed to do the trick for Mary.

Mary, in her attempt to live down the end of town she came from, had actually found a source of strength in standard English. She had come to realize in herself a basic function and measure of literacy:

> I can say "that's not right." It's good when you can pick things out, right? When somebody, in speech, can pick out the wrong mistake, then you know you know something.

But in spite of this fundamental sense of competence, as well as a very positive attitude towards books and literature ("27. Literature—is great. I love it"), Mary's langauge continued to be under a form of indirect assault in her classes:

> They do it all the time. In history, teachers always ask, like, what are your marks in English. They also look at your grammar. They always ask who's your teacher in English class. ("Do they correct your speech?") Not always, sometimes they catch onto what you're saying.

She has begun, much like Ralph and Jane, to subscribe to the idea that "correction" implies incoherence and senselessness. (Why else would the teachers pursue it?) Mary is also like the other two in her unquestioning acceptance of the value of schooling and the authority of its judgements. Yet both Mary and Jane, in their final year of high school, have preserved a source of strength, a belief in themselves, to run against being "west end" or "tongue-tied." Mary, for her part, felt that having a specific goal distinguished her:

> 1. When I'm 25 I expect to be—an Accountant that have successful graduated from Business School.

Jane had a sense of her own capabilities outside of language. Ralph had less than that. He mentioned his interest in sports, but saw little future in it. This lack of a point of strength and defence may be because he is still in the middle of the process, stalled for a second year in grade ten. This year and Ms. MacLeod had, however, made a difference for Ralph:

> 38. What has made my life clearer to me is—that I now know I can really be smart if I tried.

What this meant, he explained in the interview, was that in "the first term [of the school year] I seen my grades were good [in English], that's the reason I seen that I could." One cannot realize these matters on one's own; they must be certified, granted or denied. Ms. MacLeod later told me that the second term would be a poor one for Robert, as a result of his sporadic attendance and incomplete assignments.

These things come and go.

The distinction between the two ends of town was considered by quite a few students to be a racial one: "when you say west end a lot of people think black, instantly they think black" (Bob, 12Gm:19). But it was less often conceived of in terms of language differences, at least directly so. The differences in achievement and stream placement, for example, were explained in terms of attitudes, poor junior highs and on occasion institutional discrimination:

> 9. One contradiction in this school is—that everybody is supposed to get equal education but the blacks are usually steered to general courses instead of academic. (12Am:30)

An alternative to these common sense explanations was provided by Chris who saw the differences as flowing out of the politics of language. He was a white general level grade twelve student. There is no doubt that he was unusually sensitive to my interests in this research; he had, for instance, spoken with me about my work in the hall after classes on a couple of occasions. However with that in mind, his perceptiveness did seem to extend beyond a reading and perhaps a slight dramatizing of the concerns of this interviewer:

> There's a little war going on, in case you haven't noticed—west and east end. There are some people in the east end using their word power against the west end. The east enders will try to talk you out of it, use psychological points of view and beat you down.

Chris saw it very much as a language and power issue. It was what Mary was hinting at, and what she was admonishing against—"we shouldn't put ourselves down." Chris seemed more inclined to specify and judge the force that needs resisting:

> The flow of the east end—they're going a bit overboard towards the use of English; they're actually losing reality. . . . They flow into the theory of the school. Some of it has to do with power, dealing with their fathers; cause a lot of power is in the east end and it can affect the west end.[4]

Chris believes, however, that he is at a decided advantage in this war; one of the main things he has learned about language "is how to use word power." It is most useful, he explained, when you are called to the office of the vice-principal:

> I know exactly what he is going to say and have something to countersay before he even gets in there. So he says "O.K., go."

Chris is repeating grade twelve, but he is sure "you can look at marks and they ain't going to show you a thing" ("I say 'ain't' once in awhile—that's the only thing [wrong] I say"). He remains confident and above the processes he perceives. He is one of the students who keeps his ski jacket on in class. It was his comment on school 'as pure theory' which provides an epigraph for this chapter. Part of his strength and the belief he has in himself derive from his relationship to language— "I use English; I pick everything out of English I want." The reason for this, I am speculating, is a special literary practice; he has the expanded forum which, for example, a number of academic students said they required if they were to achieve greater self-expression. In Chris's case the forum is music:

> I'm in a [rock music] group; I write the lyrics for the songs and I have to be able to have information at the tips of my fingers. . . . I have to be able to relate it to words. . . . I get into political stuff as well but you can't pick the stuff out, I just put it into my words; it hits you psychologically. You can really say we use our English when it comes to things like that.

When it comes to things like that you can see how use of language gives him a sense of power, intellectual power—he is "using" his English, and he is not about to be used badly by it. He seems quite protected from what he might otherwise have come to understand about himself and the force of his words. Whether his band ever gets out of his basement, he has written for it and the band has backed and amplified what he has had to say. That it has put him in a rather special relation to language was indicated on the SCT. He was the only male and the only general level student to state that he was most careful about his language (item 26) in terms which suggested something of a literary concern: "—when I write a letter (song, poem) to my girlfriend." The band is comparable to Edward's never-quite-to-be literary magazine; it provides a common concern for a kind of language—a community of discourse—beyond the realm and the reach of red circling and scores out of twenty. One can see, though, that Chris has had to go farther than Edward to believe in his own literacy; the failed year, the general level and his problems with the school would more thoroughly deny what Chris believes he has—word power. The music has afforded him a spot beyond what is commonly regarded as "general level," "west ender," or "repeater." One of the important differences this word power makes in Chris' eyes is the ability to face up to the authority of the school, as a west ender:

> This is more like east end school. A west ender may come in [to the vice-principal's office]. They haven't got the word power the school's expecting and they're—Mr. Brewster [the vice-principal]—they're going to get upset by the use of words and start getting sarcastic. . . . Ya, they tried it to me, but it don't work.

To suggest, as I have, that Chris' song writing has contributed significantly to what he makes of himself may appear exaggerated, as might much of what he has had to say. Chris' tendency to dramatize would seem justified by the odds he is up against, and my faith in the power of music is based on the widespread use of it as a source of self-definition in the school. This is, of course, not unique to Kipling, it is rather part of what distinguishes youth culture. At Kipling it serves in a struggle of identities which is played out, principally, on the laminated maple desk-tops. The tops are conveniently sanded clean each year and left unvarnished for a fresh graffiti war between exponents of punk, rock, and disco music. The battle of the bands is then crudely scratched into the wood, though in places it is carefully etched in the manner of corporate logos. More interesting perhaps were the desk-top dialogues that would advise and explore standards. On the top of one desk:

> I'm not a slug just because I like The Who. I don't wear a jean jacket or hang around the front door or smoke, do drugs or get wasted all the time.
>
> Punk sure isn't as commercial as the shit you must listen to .
>
> I suppose you don't even like the Beatles.
>
> **Be Yourself Ass!** And stop putting down other people because of what they like. (Ms. McLeod's classroom)

After a first snowfall in December "DEVO," a "new-wave" band, was stamped out across the front yard of the school in a bold if temporary display of identification. Pop music is a statement against the school, or at least a form of power quite beyond its grasp. Though, as it turns out, it is still very much a part of the "class system," as one student referred to it. A classmate of Chris' pointed out how this, in effect, worked:

> At the dances all they [east enders] play is punk music. A lot of people from the west end like rock so they won't go at all. Most of the people on student council that work at the dances are from the east end. (12Gf:05)

Music is a point of focus and force; it does not, as one might ideally imagine, take them into a universal form of communication that somehow unites as it delights, but it can put the world, such as it is, into their own terms. It is for these reasons that I believe in the importance of Chris writing the songs his band will sing. It would be too much, perhaps, to suggest it is responsible for his perceptiveness, but it would seem unwise not to recognize the kind of support he draws from it:

> I find people who are more creative get away from the standard English. (Chris)
>
> . . . and his heart was going like mad and yes I said yes I will Yes. (James Joyce)

Finally, I would point out that this rock literacy of Chris' had not gone completely to his head. He could still be unsure and painfully realistic; word power has its limits:

> 1. When I'm 25 I expect to be—an artist or a dry-wall worker.

There are many points of strength and susceptability on this issue of language distinctions at Kipling. I wish to include one further student from the general level, if only because his singular point of strength is his degree of literacy, a literacy which he gratefully acknowledged as the work of the school:

> If you start reading books you enjoy it more than television or anything like that. What I always do is, I want to pick in on a character I like the most and then live in the part of the character as he goes through the book. . . .
>
> I like to put my thoughts down on paper; it's interesting to see how, the way I think—"like wow, I think that, wow pretty weird." . . . I get ideas for stories and someday I'll probably do a book. (Bob, 12Gm:19)

It had not always been this way. Bob went through what might be viewed as a literacy conversion in grade 10. He gives credit to a single teacher, and the conversion is surely the best one might hope for from an English program. The redemption was from out of the darkness of a poorly-grasped language and into the glory that is literature. Chris provided quite a tribute to the efforts of his grade ten teacher, Mr. Avis, and to how much is really at stake:

> I always had bad marks in all my classes in junior high because I felt so self-conscious of "I did wrong," you know, "oh no." Most of the time I would end up not doing it at all because I was afraid of doing it wrong and writing it down wrong because my grasp of the English language was so poor. When I got in grade 10 I had Mr. Avis and he improved my language 100%. ("How?") A lot of reading. . . . I'm very sports minded but I found it quite relaxing. . . . I'd read a book and I'd feel calm and relaxed. I always thank Mr. Avis for that because I always figured it was really Mr. Avis that introduced me into reading and hence into English, into standard English.

But somehow the conversion was not enough. It has certainly made Bob a literate concern, but it has still not given him the confidence to enroll in an English course at the academic level.[5] His choice of a general level class doesn't have to be viewed as a failure, though his enthusiasm for literature does make him appear miss-streamed. The explanation he provided for his choice of general level, in fact, is in terms of its literate offering (and quite in contrast to notions of the "dumping ground"):

> Mr. Russell's class [12G] is geared a lot to reading. I was told when I signed up
> for general, it's geared a lot toward reading. There's some writing, but not as
> much as you will encounter in academic.

And thus we arrive at the flaw in Bob's literacy, the lingering legacy of his pre-literate days, which prevents him from making more of his interests and abilities in reading:

> I like to write, but I have very very bad spelling, really, and that frustrates me a
> lot. . . . The reason I went into that [general level] is because I read well, and
> writing assignments in regular [academic] English—you get the mistakes and
> you lose points.

Of course, Mr. Russell takes points off too—"up to half marks" in a question—but Bob believes "its not so much how you put it down" at the general level and that he, given this limitation, can still do well. He had eighteen spelling errors on the forty items of the SCT; he missed, for example, "envious," "surprisingly," "informative," and "their." He is not exaggerating the case with his spelling; it is somewhat out of phase with the rest of his literary development. But while he seemed to write without a great deal of concern over the issue—he used words he had little idea of how to spell—it definitely dogged his efforts and his sense of literacy:

> No doubt if I could write, if I could spell perfectly and grammar and everything
> like that I'd be writing a mile a minute—I'd probably have a book by now. . . . I
> love to write, I love the ideas.

The very conception of this possibility—to "have a book"—would seem central, however vaguely daydreamed about, to an enthusiasm for literacy. These ideas are, of course, often given up and come to seem adolescent, but it is the very adolescent nature of this daydream which points to its special importance, at this stage, in the formation of a literate self. There is imagined the possibility of participation in this expressive form of life—to fully find oneself in print. Bob aspires to this degree of literacy and has a remarkably strong sense of literacy's worth. The fact is it can happen in a general level class. Not only that, Bob saw it receiving both instruction and support from Mr. Russell:

> Does the approach to reading [used in his class]. . . help? Definitely, definitely
> helps a lot. I pick up characterization now in books that I would never have
> picked up before I took like, advanced literature [grade 12 general]. Usually it
> was just read a book and you liked the character, but not it's "oh ya, he does
> this"—the little under-meaning now, the undercurrent.

There are also with Bob, the other classic symptoms which mark a literate concern. He judges and corrects the English of others to prove his grasp; he understands and appreciates the social advantages of using the proper form. Even with the spelling problem, even from within the general level English program, Bob has acquired a determinate sense of his literacy, and how it can serve him:

> Everybody wants a certain amount of respect from people and if you can't talk to people or come off as being stupid you just don't get that respect from people. . . . I personally pride myself on being able to talk to a wide range of people . . . being able to talk to them the way they want to be talked to.

There is that element of deference, to the point of diffidence, with Bob. He is grateful for what literacy and for what the school have done for him. Yet it is, of course, the school which has also given Bob the sense of his limitations, located specifically in his spelling; he doesn't suspect or question, for instance, the way Chris does. Bob is curious, intellectually so, but he is also concerned and anxious to please. Bob's literacy is, by his own account, flawed, and it may be quite fatally so in terms of opening up new worlds for him. The book may never come, though one expects he will remain an avid reader. He will, however, always understand his literacy as shallow, limited to a kind of affability: "being able to talk to them." He will remain very sensitive to the fact that he will have to watch, lest he gives himself away:

> I'd like to be in a job where I'd be able to talk to people . . . less writing than possible . . . . I'm going to try to coach . . . . That's not so much writing as communicating with people. . . . The writing becomes extremely minimal and I definitely want a job with people.

14. Students in the general English classes—do not have an understanding or appreciation of how important English is. (Annie, 10Af:69)

I would hope that I have made it apparent how wrong Annie is about this at its deepest level; what she reads, accurately enough, is the message the students and teachers of the general program ostensibly deliver to the rest of the school. Yet, the general level students can hardly convince themselves of it, in many cases. If it were true, the significance of standard English would not be as it is, and would not mean what it does for the students I have just discussed. However, Annie's statement, as it reflects on the "understanding or appreciation" of academic students, will serve as a focus for considering the students from that program.

What Annie appreciates about the importance of English is, as with most students, mixed; but what it unmistakeably centres around is the earning and expecting of a certain respect; it is to secure your place in those special places:

> Standard English I think is easier to understand. When you go to a fancy restaurant, that's what you're expected to use. . . . When you go to a nice clothes store that is what you're expected to use. . . . When you have to get formal you need it and its good to have. . . . English to me is something like manners.

The way she began with ease of understanding and ended with manners should be kept in mind. The intelligibility may appear to be an ideological frill, yet it provides ballast should the fancy business of manners seem too flimsy. Annie's concern with standard English, as a point of judgement, still requires a basis of some sort—manners must mean something more than arbitrary adherence to formalities: "I've noticed people who don't particularly use good English. . . . I sort of get the impression they haven't been raised properly, maybe they don't care, you know."

It is a sense she is making, not of the language, but of the tremendous concern with judgement. She found this atmosphere of linguistic distinctions and judgements quite pervasive. She thought that the teachers "try to be fair to everybody and they don't judge people by talking." But she realized, on saying this, that it was ith grace and some style. The teacher did "bother" with her. She had developed an assertive manner that was intended not to offend. You might recall that this was something Ralph was interested in establishing with his teacher, Ms. MacLeod, though he had yet to find the right tone.

There is one element noticeably absent from Annie's sense of the importance of English. Her account of literacy is one in which books play little part. With regard to the reason English teachers promote "literature," she was quite unsure: "Maybe they think it's good reading material and they want us to become familiar with it." Books too becomes a matter of being raised properly. As for her own interests she found herself "so caught up reading novels for English class" that she read little outside of these school demands. In her regard for writing, she seemed boldly free of concerns with decorum, though there was still recourse to the standards of social approval, even in what seemed to be a strong stand against saccharine and classroom propriety:

> I don't try to make up a cute little story that the teacher will like. I just go for what happened to me and the way I feel. Mr. Smith likes that because he knows it's coming from us. I don't worry too much about punctuation or spelling, I just sit down and write. . . . I've got O.K. marks from him. They're pretty good. I think that's what he wants.

She seems to have an excellent grasp of James Britton's "expressive" writing mode which Mr. Smith was encouraging in her class; she clearly makes the point I raised before that there can be little writing "for yourself"—the intention of expressive writing—among students who do not ask themselves is this "what he wants?"

Annie understood that her language distinguished her: "I go to a fancy restaurant; I feel its my duty to sound this way. . . . Well, you get better service" (which might be compared to Mr. Russell's comments cited above on duty and TV personality, George Jefferson). But is was also a matter of class location, a case of distinguishing the end of town one was from. The reference to duty is a reference to the vigilance necessary in maintaining the distinctions. Annie is black, and this seemed to confuse people as to her location in their scheme of things:

> This year I've got a lot of people saying to me, "Are you from the east end?" [the "high class" end]. They think you live in the east end just because you know how to talk to them, because you know how to relate to some of their problems. You have to prove something to them.

Notice how she has interpreted their question in such a positive light. She has had to overcome what others in the general level classes have had to live with, and she was doing it through, at least in part, standard English—"how to talk to them." The importance of English for Annie is in the self-respect which it affords. She has realized that she can find it, and that she needs it more from the faces she meets than from the books she might read:

> You fit into the class you're comfortable with. I just think standard English is important because it gives you more respect and it makes you feel good about yourself.

She did, on one occasion, place standard English on another plane: "Learning it, I think, is going to improve your intelligence." But this, along with the quiet pleasures of literature, are secondary to the social struggle she perceived:

> I've seen a lot of jealousies in this school. The lower class trying to beat up on, pick up on the other class. They wouldn't be jealous unless maybe they know their limitations. Maybe they know they're not exactly using standard English and that they can never, that they won't be accepted by this certain group because they don't.

Though Annie is principally concerned with forming the right social impression with her English, she is not cynical about it. In terms of Erving Goffman's original descriptions of social impression management, we have in Annie one who both believes it is all a routine to be used to obtain related ends, and yet would also seem quite sincere, or "taken in," by her own display (Goffman 1959, p. 18 ff.). To "improve your intelligence" is an aspect of this latter position. She is drawing on the lore and ideology of the language form; it is not what she needs or expects from it, but it serves her belief in its importance.

Yet I find that the sincerity of her concern with impression management suggests something deeper than a "presentation of self"—than the "fronts" and "performances" in which Goffman frames the world—though there is undoubtedly an element of this in the language skills she is acquiring. She is, at this point, and along with many of her classmates, **constructing** a self. It is a much more arduous and demanding task than its subsequent presentation will prove to be . Goffman speaks of individuals as performers "concerned not with the moral issue of realizing these standards, but with the amoral issue of engineering a convincing impression that these standards are being realized" (p. 251). There is certainly a sense of this in many of the students, but with Annie it is a moral quest for "respectability," for "acceptance," and as a matter of "duty." It is equally a moral and penetrating concern for some of the other students who know they have no valid or viable performance to present. Ralph and Jane, for instance, believe in the act they cannot give; it has, in their estimation, left them speechless.

Annie has found a voice then. She is a literate concern, though not very much of a literary one. She has seen reason enough in the world to believe in the importance of standard English; it is part of what she will make of herself, of what she would be: "I guess I'm—very hopeful and expect a lot from life."

Edward's comments on literature and writing have already been used in the preceding two chapters; he seemed to represent a kind of high literacy with his very effective defence of literature and his dedication to writing. I do not wish to repeat these aspects of his position but add to them his view on language differences. He makes a few distinctions which would increase our understanding of his regard for standard English. On the question of why some students use standard English and some nonstandard, he is in a position to drop what so many others seemed to need: "I don't think it's related to intelligence; it's related to the class structure that we all live in." He situates this class structure geographically in the town and he situates it racially, as so many did. But there still is a basic difference, if only in what he grants to these other students. He has attempted to shift the focus from capabilities to the social situation and identity:

> For instance, there's a very distinct black way of talking. It's completely different from the way east enders talk. . . . I think it has to do with the way they relate to themselves and I suppose it's the same way with east enders. It's a form of their identity, a rebelliousness. . . . In the sort of prestige things, if that has any meaning, the east enders dominate the school. (Edward, 12Am:33)

It does, of course, have meaning for many of the students. It speaks to the rebelliousness of some and the snobbery of others ("especially what they talk about—a lot of social climbing: 'I went skiing this weekend' "). Edward is somewhat detached. He has, then, found a position half-a-step back from the situation; it is the same with students from his end of town, "east enders" and it is a matter of identity, dominance and class. But he is still beginning from a sense of the black students' "complete" difference.

Edward, though he willingly took the teachers' "line" on literature (see chapter 3), has not taken schooling nor his success therein so thoroughly at its word. The secret of a student's success in English, he indicated on item 20, is "due to middle class value system," or more plainly, "my dad's a doctor—I think that affects the way people talk." The privilege of Edward's literacy is really in this sense which it affords, that sometimes it isn't "**just** a line they've been handing us" and that sometimes it is nothing more than that. The school has not been able to raise in his the same sensitivities and anxieties that the other students must always be so artfully dodging or taking broadside.[6] He made no more than a passing reference to standard English as a matter of presenting oneself—"the practical reasons," as he referred to the matter which had so concerned the others. He has been able to distance himself from his education with more credibility than most, (though he too at times stood in contradiction to this):

> 11. All this schooling will—in the long run be forgotten having had no effect whatsoever.

Other students said as much (there were 16% negative responses to the item), but with Edward it is his literacy, combined with his sense of class position, which created the possibility that the rest of it will be so forgettable and ineffective.

There were other instances of this distancing of oneself from the school, but more often there was a great deal of faith expressed in it. There is reason to believe that faith expressed may be the sufficient if not the necessary element of success at Kipling. Lisa was an enriched grade twelve English student who exemplifies this leap; it is an ingenuous faith, though not without depth or substance. Her central tenet was: "you always learn something from books" (twice mentioned in the interview; once on the SCT). Yet her explanation of why English teachers might put such an emphasis on literature betrayed just how much of a matter of faith it can be:

> I suppose it's been pretty popular for that long, there must have been something to it; most of it is pretty old. Because you can always learn something from a

book. . . . Because people who wrote were really smart and you can learn a lot
from them. . . . [laughter] Shakespeare's pretty famous. (Lisa, 12Af:38)

She was, however less sure and even quite dubious about the inclusion of the
metaphysical poets in the curriculum:

> You're taking such a small group of people who were so enclosed, narrow-
> minded and everything . . . and you feel so left out.

The pleasure she gets out of reading—"I love books; I read all the time"—
seems quite unspoiled or unaffected by all of the appreciation which literature
received in the enriched class. She is not involved or engaged by it. Though she
does well by it—"I just freaked when I got 80[%]"—it does not seem to be very much
a product of the first requirement for the enriched class, enthusiasm:

> You're supposed to choose a poem and write five pages; its going to be bull
> probably. . . . then you have to talk about the stuff that's in all poems like
> syntax, whatever that is. . . .

What she was much clearer about is the right tone to take: "You have to sound
like you know what you're talking about." There was a time before she had learned
this lesson: "They [her classmates] were saying 'What **was** he [Mr. Allen] talking
about today?'" But now the proper approach for the perplexed seems clear: "Some
will sit there and just pretend—like I know they do—and then they make their
points on things they understand." The other dimension to this successful literacy
without literature is a fundamental competence in the basics of standard English:
"it was just drilled into me when I was little." Competence remains a point of
distinction and justification with her: "14. Students in the general English classes—
have never learned the basics and are learning them now." But she also responded
to my question on her writing with an immediate, "I stink at writing":

> I'm great at getting information but I can't make it stick together. Teachers
> always put "awkward," "too long a sentence" and I'm kind of working on it but
> it's weird.

The judgements of the school are taken as the point of reference, which stands
in contrast with Edward's comment, "When I do write I expect it to be as good as the
things I read." In the evaluation of the assignment mentioned above—"you have to
choose a poem"—Mr Allen directed his comments in the fashion she suggested he
would, to the misleading, meandering, and awkward. He, too, in his response to
this piece of literature appreciation, seemed to be suggesting that ultimately you
had to "sound like you know." In this case, "to sound like you know" is to place the
dependent clause with the right relative pronoun in the proper spot:

> . . . Bermuda has the most beautiful cedars in the world **that are yellow, brown, red, and purple** ("Bermuda," Lisa' Mr. Allen's emphasis).
>
> Misleading—seems only its yellow, brown . . . cedars are the most beautiful (Mr. Allen's comment, including his ellipsis).

This awkwardness is handled, however, in an incidental and individual manner, rather than as a general deficiency of the class which required regular remedial lessons. Yet fidelity to form is still a particular concern at the enriched level, in the "intensive" and "enthusiastic" study of literature. There can still be an absorption in form and manoeuvring, essentially, in "sounding like." It has influenced Lisa's sense of her literacy—"I stink." It will shape what and how she writes until "sounding like" doesn't count anymore, though perhaps it always will.

Yet when the 'bull," Lisa had picked Marvell's poem, "Bermuda," because she, too, had arrived at the island by boat in a similar thankful-unto-God mood:

> Like when we're on the boat and you come through something, everybody doesn't kind of kneel down and pray, but I **always** say something to myself even if I don't always go to church.

This connection, unfortunately, gets lost somewhere, sacrifice to the assignment which takes on a check-list approach to imagery, rhythm, diction, and finally, irony. It is interesting, too, how she misinterpreted the task. The final aspect of it she told me was "to write why you like it." Mr. Allen laughed on hearing this; he told me the final question was, rather, "How is it great poetry?" And there lies the difference—to objectify why **you** like it into why **it** is "great"; to shift the justification of the judgement to the qualities of the object. It is the distance which Lisa still has to travel, leaving her family and boat behind. She accepts that; she sees no "unlearning" or "forcing of an appreciation" as others had. Where she might have connected—truly in Mr. Smith's "expressive" sense—she has misunderstood the assignment. But she's "working on it," getting out the **Handbood on Literature** from the library and attending to those comments (well almost—"Mr. Allen doesn't really help, he just puts comments").

Lisa's attitude towards language differences accedes to the common elements of concern:

> Sometimes teachers might just think you're automatically dumber too. I'd rather speak the way I do . . . if you go some place really special then you get dressed up. . . .

It is reminescent of Annie's position, though over the course of the interview Lisa proved less anxious about these concerns. It is similarly a literacy without literature. The association between standard English and the "really special" or the fancy restaurant presents what they understand as their most demanding linguistic moments, as if this were an important part of what they could properly be—as women. Standard English, has been prescribed to them as part of their dressing up for the world; it is, however, still going to leave them without the full power of the form—it is for show, but not to tell. Lisa shared Annie's sense of independence: "8. What makes me different is—I don't do what everyone else does" (Lisa); "no one is like me" (Annie). But Lisa, like Annie, recognized literacy as, ultimately, her duty:

> But if you're in university, paying to go there or if you've got a scholarship, if you've worked that hard then you should know how to write it [standard English]. Like when people put the apostrophe in the wrong place, that's pitiful!

"The understanding or appreciation of how important English is," which Annie thought so crucial, can be found in the comments of these students. There are those who, as Chris put it, flow with the theory of the school, though I would point out that it was not just the east enders who were so fortunate. It would be difficult, for example, to exclude Ralph or Jane form this category. They, too, are caught up in the flow and have indeed taken the school's designations seriously; they believe they are loud, sassy and inarticulate. But at the other end of this rather profound reading of the consequences of language differences are Annie and Lisa, equally in tune with the theory, yet concerned with the superficial nature of language forms— "fitting in comfortably" and "sounding like." There is quite a distance between these two positions—from the profound to the superficial; from intelligence and articulation to social impression and duty—though in their way they remain equally sensitive to the importance of standard English. The students would seem to move toward the superficial aspects of language, the concerns with membership and participation, as they increase their command of standard English. But how is one to account for this shift in significance for those caught up in the theory of the school?

I would speculate that this difference is based, at least in part, on the discourse and materials with which the students have to work. I do not mean by materials, "ability" or "competence," but the messages and the responses which they have been receiving from the school, though by no means exclusively through that medium. Quite simply, Ralph and Jane have learned that they are missing something, either the words or the ability to do well. Because the distinctions are blurred by the evaluations of teachers, they have little choice but to believe it is both. In the school, ability and expression are associated with competency in standard English, and that fact is reflected in Ralph's and Jane's sense of their own inadequacy, their sense of linguistic failure.

The situation for Annie and Lisa in the advanced academic classes has been more promising, and they have become more realistic about the significance of language forms. The message for them has been that they have the ability and the language—hence their "enriched" position—but that their mastery of the form, which is paramount, is still in a rough and awkward state. They appreciate the importance of this and have indicated that they are working on it. But more importantly they seem to understand that they are, and must continue to be, deserving of this special status—both in the school and downtown—by virtue of their ability to rise to the occasion with style, either in language or clothing. It seems incumbent on them, in light of their sense of status, to act properly; they both expressed a sense of duty towards the use of standard English.

Finally, there is a third position, quite apart from this continuum which flows with the school, from the profound to the superficial significance of standard English. Chris and Edward have found a way of distancing themselves from this process. They recognize the power of the school and of the language form, but they are not as willing to take hold of its "line" or "theory." Just so, they would participate, using their word power, but they have a frame of reference and support, whether in music, literary groups or social class position, to remain outside of the school's jurisdiction in certain matters of judgement. More secure and less anxious about the school's view of them, they have proven less susceptible to, for example, the ascription of inherent abilities over language differences, especially when they find class, politics and power provide better explanations for the distinctions which are made.

If I were to place Mary and Bob, both half-believing in their literacy and the school, it would be somewhere on the original continuum between the profound and the superficial. But this doesn't need to be that neatly accomplished, by twos. I have simply attempted to provide the contrasts and range in these students' positions, and demonstrate how this related to their lives in the school.

6
The Conclusion
The Well-Tempered Tongue

Why do we fail to teach the mother tongue freely, honestly, joyously?

There must be something in our society which flinches from the liberation of the whole unpredictable, perhaps unmanageable human being.

Peter Abbs

The project would seem to be complete: I have described both what the teaching of English is and what language has become for a number of teachers and students at Kipling High School. Yet to say that the school has contributed, by intention and ommission, to the greater articulation of some of the students and to the silencing of others, is to beg corrective measures—alternative programs, revised curriculums and enlightened in-service sessions.

These are all, however, measures which have been repeatedly advised and in various forms made available over the last decade as sociolinguistics has become more of a presence in education. Linguists, for example, have been constant in recommending teacher-preparation courses on the nature and social context of language (Cazden 1971; Bullock 1975; Macaulay 1977). Yet what becomes clear in examining the available materials is that the texts have not gone as far nor as deep as the attitudes which I found among students and teachers. To consider one possible example which might be used with teachers, there is R. E. McConnell's recent **Our Own Voice: Canadian English and How It Is Studied** (1979). For the most part the book focuses, as is our wont in this broad land, on geographical differences, particularly in vocabulary and accent. It does include half a page on the "Social Dimensions" of dialect variations; she notes that "Canada, too, has its social dialects, and in spite of a hundred years of public education, its lingering linguistic shibboleths" (p. 102). Yet, the discussion of these shibboleths goes no further than to suggest: "Gauge your own reactions, for instance, if someone says, 'It don't' or 'He done it good' " (ibid.).

There have also been language textbooks produced for the Canadian classroom which address the history of the language and the situation of dialects. Henderson and Shepard's text, **Language Matters** (1975), which, while strangely given over to preparing students to write advertising copy, does provide the senior high class with at least one lesson on dialects: "Dialect creates its own vocabulary—one that is often richer and more evocative than commonplace English" (p. 124). But while they grant a certain dignity to dialects as the "uncommon" and thus a useful resource, the question of how variations are maintained and exploited does not arise. McMaster, in a more recent text. **Communicating in Your World** (1979), goes further; he includes a short history of the language which begins promisingly: "In the seventeenth and eighteenth centuries, the English grammarians appeared, devoting themselves to 'refining, ascertaining, and fixing' the language" (p. 161). But this act of "acertaining" is made to seem the result of an earlier ignorance about the nature of language, an ignorance which we have subsequently overcome: language, we now realize, "is a growing evolving thing . . . it cannot be fixed without killing it" (p. 163). This approach again does little to address the experience and consequences of language differences and language fixing which I found among speakers, as "growing evolving things," at Kipling High School.

There is not, in these texts, a complete denial of the elements of power and struggle in language, but there is a softening or blurring of them as both a protective measure—of the student as a child—and a defensive one—of the school as it is implicated. Out of these efforts to protect, however, there develops a deceptive portrayal of the social reality, a reality which these students have proven to know only too well:

> Some of us, through imaginative speech or writing or through holding positions of prestige affect the language more than others. But, because we think, because we do things, because we are alive, we are **all** makers and changers of language. (**Language Learning**, Penner and McConnell 1977, p. 37, original emphasis)

Finally, while Light (1977) has found that teaching against language prejudice can achieve a measure of success with eight year olds, the use of in-service sessions with teachers appears to hold less promise (as cited above, Walker et al. 1975; "Ann Arbor Results Inconclusive" 1981).

The English teachers at Kipling recognized, in an academic sense, the issue of language prejudice, the sufficiency of other dialects and the need to respect the language of their students—it is, if nothing else, provincial policy (NSDE 1972; 1978). But is was also a concern of the Language for Learning program, which Mr. Smith was promoting within the department, and which has begun to move the focus away from a concern with form, and towards self-expression. It seems quite likely, then, that these teachers are making **less** of a contribution to the use of language as a means of affirmation and exclusion than English teachers had previously, a point noted on a larger scale in English teaching by Mathieson (1975). The question is still, however, that with a teaching staff so informed and motivated, why are there still such a number of students who think so badly of their language and their ability to express themselves?

The first point to be noted is that the issue, for both students and teachers, is not an acdemic one—a matter of lessons, texts or workshops. It is, rather, a profoundly psychological one. It involves what the teachers and students have made of themselves and how they have been constituted in the language and organization of the school. These are matters of identity and self-definition, of the politics and struggle for position in the community of discourse. And these matters, within my particular focus on standard English, must be considered as people participate in a linguistic and social universe currently made up of a prestige form surrounded by a host of dialects and deviations.

But aside from the individual instances of language and limitation, this study has come upon traces of a bias which were undoubtedly directed against certain groups, against blacks, girls and west enders. Black students constituted a linguistic category for a number of the English teachers, a category which benefited these students little; girls suffered a loss of voice as an aspect of their feminine identity; and west enders were not coached in defending the case they were not considered to have. But charges of racism, sexism and social class privilege are not to be raised lightly nor simply for effect. Rather, I would use the shadow they have cast over the English program to examine how prejudice persists in an institution dedicated to equality of opportunity.

Consider the case of the black students. The black community in Nova Scotia is an old and well established one. Blacks first arrived in Nova Scotia as slaves shortly after the founding of Halifax in 1749 (Clairmount and Magill 1970). Later, as both the slaves of Loyalists and as "freemen" with military service for the British, they setled in the province at the time of the American Revolution and the War of 1812. For over two hundred years blacks have inhabited and continued to move into the province, but they have lived apart on the rocky land they were first granted for their service to the crown and in communities they built among the white population. Segregated schools in Nova Scotia lost their legislative sanction in 1954 when all references to race were removed from the province's Education Act.It was the year of the landmark Supreme Court decision on civil rights in the United States, a decision based on the rejection of separate but equal facilities for black students. Racism in education is not longer a legislated fact in Nova Scotia, but it has not been so easily eradicated from its institutions. The most political of all questions are not to be thoroughly governed by the state.

At Kipling High School, the black students hung out at the west door of the school in their time between classes. They kept apart there, as they were dept apart in the comments of the English teachers on language problems in the school. Race was maintained by the staff as a valid, deviant language category. Still the black students were streamed with other students at the general level whose language did not adhere closely enough to the standard—equal treatment but separate regard. Racial distinctions have remained a category of convenience rooted in the English teachers' professional work with the students, not just in assessing the students' language, but as well in matters of attendance and respect. Clearly, for some of the teachers, characterizations of standard English performance and attendance were made with an acceptable degree of reliability on the basis of skin color. Yet it should also be clear that denigrating racial references to the students' language and sense of order are a holdover from those earlier days in the history of the province and the continent, days of racial exploitation and latent ideologies of racial differences.

The distinctions which standard English provides in sorting the students into "college bound" or "high school leaving" courses have lent themselves to unnecessary racial distinctions. This mild but by no means benevolent regard for race turns up in the explanations which the teachers have developed for the differences in mastery of standard English and for the lack of interest in the English program. Ralph and Jane bore the marks of this racial bias in their belittling depiction of themselves as speakers. The sorting and ranking on the basis of a specific competence, whether in English, physics or volleyball, does not do the damage. The problem lies in what must be considered as the sloppy use of race as, in effect, the relevant factor or cause in deviance from the standard. Whatever the teachers' professed position on the issue of racial equality—and I believe that the four teachers I worked with were not at all racist in a traditional sense—the explanations which they employ in their trade are part of older discriminations. We might suspect that these prejudices are more easily taken up in the classroom under the pressure of maintaining standards in language and behavior, out of the frustration English teachers face when confronted by something less in their students than their own enthusiasm for literature and literary language. The impact of this pressure is what seems to underly Mr. Russell's claim that he had not been prejudiced before coming to Kipling High School.

In light of this tension which has become mixed up with language and race, the English teacher's expertise in the language must be extended to the nature of social discriminations as well as to literary ones. As the teacher avoids the issue in class, language and the teaching of language become tainted; the lesson which is not taught still suggests that the language of black students is the result of either dumbness, carelessness or defiance. The avoidance of the issue does little, we have seen, to prevent either the students from continuing to suffer these prejudices or the teachers from slipping into them in talking about their work. Prejudices in language are relevant to an education in standard English—the standard would mean little without them—and in this damaging form they should be confronted in class rather than circumvented and ignored. If unwarranted assumptions are not actively taught against, they too easily become part of the teachers' and the students' explanation for failure.

The students and the staff at the school regard standard English as a given—as "the proper," if not "the smarter," by the students, and "the way of the educated" by the staff. Standard English is not merely a scale for measurement—Fahrenheit or Celsius, effective or appropriate—but becomes the freezing point of language itself. The standard serves, in this sense, as an inherent quality of the language in its pure state. Only as the given, "effective" language form can standard English be used to accomplish what Foucault has termed "the appropriation of discourse":

> Education may well be, as of right, the instrument whereby every individual, in a society like our own, can gain access to any kind of discourse. But we well know that in its distribution, in what it permits and in what it prevents, it follows the well-trodden battle-lines of social conflict. Every education system is a political means of maintaining or of modifying the appropriation of discourse, with the knowledge and the power it carries with it. . . . What is an educational system after all, if not the ritualization of the word; if not a qualification of some fixing of roles for speakers; if not the constitution of a (diffuse) doctrinal group; if not the distribution and an appropriation of discourse, with all its learning and its powers? (Foucault 1972, p. 227)

What indeed? In this instance, it is an appropriation of propriety and respectability for some of the students; but for others it also means the appropriation of sensible speech and a credible voice. There remains little left over for the classroom except noise and silence. However, this claim on discourse is hardly left to go unchallenged.[1] The students make room for themselves between these leftover areas through, for instance, sassing, loudness and rock music, itself a kind of sassy trumpeting—blaring?—against propriety: "The concessions of **politeness** always contain **political** concessions" (Bourdieu 1977, p. 95, original emphasis). But the students resisted in a quieter and more polite fashion, as well, through indifference and a sullen silence.

As Jane and Ralph demonstrated, the appropriation can be both learned and resisted. It seems to be a negotiated settlement between the students' acknowledgement of the essential appropriation—"I know what it is but I can't explain it properly," as Jane put it—and the teachers' absorption of illicit (political) expression—the talking back, speaking out of turn or coming on too loudly. In this manner, however, their form of resistance, their reaching out for a voice which will be heard, serves to confirm the appropriation of legitimate discourse. This is most clearly the moment of hegemony; even as they continue to speak out, Jane and Ralph feel that they are speechless, babbling.

Their resistance, however, is aimed at little more than pricking a hole in the enveloping claims on language. It is a play against being silenced, but it does not constitute, in itself, a critique of the appropriation; it is not, in fact, a denial of it.[2] Paul Willis has interpreted resistance of this sort as a "partial penetration of their real conditions" which, and here the paradox appears to arise, "contributes to social reproduction in general" (1977, p. 185). Students do resist and there is an effective level of social reproduction—that much appears certain. But I am not sure that the transformation, of resistance into compliance, is a paradoxical or mystical as it might seem. The hegemony succeeds, even in the face of this speaking out, by virtue of Ralph's and Jane's decision to stick to the terms of reference which do preclude fundamental demands but not a bit of smart-assing. They are not, however, willing to risk all; that is, to chance being fully excluded, as happened in a formal sense to classmates of theirs through suspensions and expulsions. They understand the terms of their inclusion, such as it is, and go no further in challenging the determinations, except to point out to the teacher that given their speech was "hard" to understand, they still have something to say.

As well as actively resisting this attempted appropriation, there is another kind of subversion which is available. Chris and Edward, from their rather different perspectives and academic levels, have achieved an understanding, or, more graphically using Willis' term, a penetration, of the process, which tends to detract from its significance. Chris realizes that the use of standard English can represent a play for power, rather than a gift of superiority, and Edward recognizes in it the reproduction of class. Their participation is, then, less absorbing of themselves, as it is more critical; they are able to draw on a different kind of affirmation from language, which is independent of the classroom. Yet with regard to the very aims of the English program, their sense of what language has to offer is a richer and more literate one than many of the other students demonstrated.

Chris' literate concerns, for example, cuts against the notion of functional literacy which has come to mean a passive, receptive facility at decoding the demands of forms, applications and notices, and then responding to them most appropriately and effectively (Levine 1982). Chris has not responded appropriately, though he has, perhaps, responded effectively. He would use his powers of articulation and interpretation to defend himself against the flow of theory, as he puts it, against the official approbations of his behavior. His literate state has to do with an insight and a critical, articulate defence—a word power—which he freely draws on. Still, Chris hasn't had Shakespeare in his classes, nor does he read Dante on the side as Edward did. Chris' must be a literacy without the prescribed literature. His poetry is a folk poetry, a pop poetry, but it would still seem to count as composition, as a crafting in language and as an attempt at the effective use of language, the phrase currently so popular in English curriculum documents. Chris represented in the study, and, I believe, in a larger sense as well, the bounds of literacy for a good number of the less successful students. His literacy has its roots in the school, but like Edward's, it too has outgrown, if not turned against, what the school would have.

Though current critical theory has restricted its focus to the resistance of the oppressed (with a few exceptions such as found in Jean Anyon's work), it would seem, from Edward's case, that this form of subversion also occurs within the dominant group. Penetration, in perceiving the ruse, can cut across academic levels, as well as class and gender. Though it does not necessarily forge links, it does tend to undermine the power and the effectiveness of a concept like standard English. Standard English can only be worked as the prestige form, as the point of affirmation or exclusion in language, if there is the active use of, and belief in, the moral and intellectual distinctions ascribed to language differences. Cynicism, among either the dominated or dominant, does not serve hegemony; it fails to cover the use of power with platitudes.

However, what is not to be lost sight of is that these lessons on the significance of language differences, contested as they are, originated outside of and long before the chalkboards and textbooks; the attempted appropriation of the proper, the serious and the credible is a political, as well as an educational, activity which predates both the growth of public schooling and before that the development of Modern English. The use of a prestige language, as a point of distinction and a political right to power and truth, is to be found like a linguistic universal or constant throughout history (Innis 1951; Kahane and Kahane 1979). The school's specific contribution, however, lies in the widespread institutionalization of the distinctions. The language academies of Italy and France, formed in the latter part of the Renaissance, were limited to establishing what counted as correct; they could not raise the sensitivity and bring home the distinctions to every citizen with the thoroughness of mass schooling. The school is particularly adept at providing for every child in the realm a further and more precise definition of both the prestige form—exactly what linguistic markers and aspects count in this regard— and the student's position in the community of discourse—with grades and levels of schooling which appear to speak directly to matters of language and intelligence.

But, of course, the school goes much further than that in teaching the significance of linguistic distinctions, principally, as I found at Kipling High School, through streaming. For in the thrust and substance of the different classes are the teachers' and the curriculum committees' reading of the usefulness of English for the students, of their future in the language. At the general level there was the writing of resumes, the reading of "gang novels," the seeking out and correcting of faulty sentences; while at the enriched academic level there was the polishing of essays, the reading and attending to the argument of literature.

Consider the enriched academic class, for example, as it was engaged in the intensive study of literature, in the pursuit of that literary knowledge which Nabokov refers to as "pure luxury" (1980, p. 381). However, to fully examine what this provides these students with, in distinction to the others, we must introduce what Nabokov, for one, would deny—matters of class and ideology. To sully this art, however, with such political machinations is not to take from the experience of literature. It is not to refute the aesthetic and very individual response the student may have to reading—the "shiver of artistic satisfaction" (Nabokov 1980, p. 382)—nor is it to belittle the profound and moving evocation which Mr. Allen, in his sonorous eloquence, achieved in certain of his classes on Donne, Shakespeare and Webster. Though a number of the enriched students were still unsure of the value of literature, they did have the opportunity to find more of themselves, a fuller sense of themselves and of the world through literature; it can provide and affirm. The critical context I wish to intrude with is how the study of literature excludes, in the streams, in the society, in its contribution to the significance of standard English.

This argument comes, in part, from the work on the "production" of literature by Etienne Balibar and Pierre Macherey (1981). They locate the ideology of literature in the distinction it lends to the well-tempered tongue, and to the linguistic distinctions which are made by the schools. Literary language, they hold, is implicated in the bourgeois installation of the dominant language form (p. 89). At the very least, the standard is represented, for all of the students, as the highest and most perfect form of expression in language. In the lessons which I witnessed the standard actually gained more by the very fact that literature is not often treated as a crafting in language, but, as simply, a text to be made sense of and to interpret. What tends to be lost is the fact that language, in its entire range, is something which can be worked to great effect, rather than just used properly, by the rules.[3] Though Mr. Smith does, in fact, point out Shakespeare's use of "bring" where it sould be "take," and Scott Fitzgerald's manuscript spelling errors, more often the authors stand, if only implicitly, as a form of celebrity endorsement for the standard form. It is, ultimately, to affix prestige to propriety.

Literature is further involved in this differentiation. Through it, Balibar and Macherey argue, "the educated dominant class" gain a " 'freedom' to think within ideology, a submission which is experienced and practiced as a mastery"; for the rest:

> They find in reading [literature] nothing but the confirmation of their inferiority: subjection means domination and repression by the literary discourse of a discourse deemed "inarticulate" and "faulty" and inadequate for the expression of complex ideas and feelings. (1981, p. 96)

Balibar and Macherey grant nothing to literature in their own style and, after the fashion of Althusser with whom they both have worked, they both would seem to grant too much to the determinations of ideology. General students did, for example, read and think of themselves as readers—they took from books—but equally so they recognized literature as a point of their distinction and inferiority. There was a clamor one day in Mr. Russell's general level class to read **Macbeth**, excerpts of which were in the anthology they were using. He succeeded in putting them off it: "they don't know they can't read Shakespeare" (Mr. Russell, January 13). I suspect, however, that they do know, though I'm not sure that they "can't" read him. The enriched, on the other hand, had no doubts that they could, though they didn't express that much interest in it. There were, however, strong indications from the students of Kipling that these different senses—of mastery and of inadequacy—had arisen along the lines of the school's divisions, much as Renee

Balibar has found more formally instituted in France (1974).

The students in the enriched academic class were immersed in a discourse of discernment, literary and moral. This is in contrast to an evaluative atmosphere more often focused on the students in the general level classes, particularly on their language; it is not surprising, then, that general level students, like Mary and Bob, believed they had mastered the language because they could readily judge others wrong. In the enriched class, the students judged the morality of literary characters and the range of human possibility in literary texts. One can imagine a different sense of authority emerging out of these lessons, as matters of style and culture, of discernment and distinction, become entangled in larger questions of guilt and responsibility. It is the point of these classes that the students learn to make these judgements with a show of confidence and competence, whether the text be **Macbeth**, the play, or Macbeth, the man. This is the point of their "freedom" and "mastery." There is nothing incidental to this discourse in the enriched class, as there certainly was in the discussions of the law, morality and justice held in the general level grade ten, which arose, for instance, on two occasions in the taking up of tests. The distinction between academic and general, based on an initial competency in standard English and and "enthusiasm" for literature, becomes a moral distinction with profound implications.

The approach to language used in the general level, however justified by attitudes prevelent in the marketplace, robbed language of significance in two ways. The first of these was a denigration of the language which the students have grown up with and which continues to be the medium of expression in their family and community. This complaint has become a commonplace over the course of the last decade, and at least one group of English teachers (Conference on College Composition and Communication 1974) has responded with a resolution declaring a "Students' Right to Their Own Language" (though they have recently experienced something of a change of heart: see Sledd 1983). But after a decade of such concerns, students were still learning that much of what they say was wrong, that their speech was somehow ineffective communication as if it were something of a non-language, though their daily experience with it would have surely denied this.

But as well as the general level class having taken from the students' language, where it should have given, the focus on grammar and surface features reduced language to the expression and communication of adherence to form. Language and literacy were transformed into a deference to propriety, of sounding as if you went to school and took it very seriously. Other conceptions of language cannot help but be waylaid by this singular regard for form at the general level.

Conceptions of the expressive power of language were at stake, along with language's ability to initiate and accomplish activities, to move people by words alone. The students' outspokeness was to be contained in class, rather than redirected, and language as a challenge to the ways of the world was not so much excluded as buried beneath what counted in the assessment of students.

At the enriched academic level, the concern with language at least approached these more powerful conceptions of language. Both in class and assignments, the students were encouraged to argue convincingly, if not with conviction, the merits of a king's course of action (in **Macbeth**) or a lover's seductive plea (in Donne's "The Flea"). They were coached from the sidelines and the margins, to make their cases coherent and persuasive, that their position could not be easily denied. As mentioned, there were conventions and formalities still to be mastered at this level. Lisa had told me that the secret of success at the enriched level was "to sound like you know what you're talking about," which is a convention of sorts. Though reminiscent of the "sounding dumb" comment at the general level, it still spoke to an expectation among enriched students of a substance to their language, of at least having something to say. The enriched academic students were assumed by their teachers to have an argument to make; they were expected to judge and to use language ably to defend those judgements.

Thus it is that I would argue that the enriched students were accorded a respect in language by their teachers which differs on a moral level from the regard paid to students at the general level. The enriched students were to be entrusted with both the language and the power of judgement. With the mechanics of the standard in hand and their commitment established, the language was regarded as theirs, and the faults they will become skilled in detecting were those of kings and lovers. At the general level, the students' language, as it met and missed the ways of the standard, was the focus of judgement whether in the exercises which were designed to represent the students' faults or in a more direct manner. The students at the general level had to prove their language was becoming more conventional, rather than their ideas more persuasive. Their language was the point of judgement, and at best they might turn this around to the point where they were able to detect the errors of others. The general level students were saddled with what is believed to be the subject of their indifference, while the best of the academic students were to pursue the object of their enthusiasm.

The concentration of the enriched class on the who and how of guilt and motive, on the development of a well-armed position from which to argue the significance of literary lives, can also be imagined to encourage a greater sense of moral authority in these students than was available to students in the general level clases. "The classic defence of literary study," Lionel Trilling has written, "holds that, from the mobilising and liberalising of the sentiments which the study of literature brings about, there results, or can be made to result, an improvement in the intelligence, and especially the intelligence as it touches the moral life" (1965, p. 4). More recently, George Grant has noted that literature has supplanted theology and philosophy as the nobel calling of the educated mind (1983). In the enriched academic class, the students were initiated into the exclusive and (to many of the students with whom I spoke) mystifying ways of literature. The benefits to the intelligence as it touches the moral life amounted to a different encouragement in language; it had become the students' right to view language as the means of making literary and moral judgements. In the presence of literature, the students would first grow thoughtful and then wise.

But this advantage which they were believed to have earned extends beyond literature and art. The students were also being encouraged in the art of rhetoric though literature and the literary essay. At the root of democracy in ancient Greece, a training in art of persuasion was first conceived as essential for participation in the governing of the state. James Kinneavy, who would restore rhetoric to the English curriculum, has expressed this as the need "to train citizens to be persuasive in a political environment" (1982, p. 21). As he notes, rhetoric has fallen from grace in the schools. But here in the enriched English class, the students were receiving some measures of preparation for a greater participation in the **polis**. This training was not equally distributed among the Greeks, nor is it yet in the modern high school. One group of students has had their attention directed to the avoidance of errors, an inducement to silence, while another was prompted to develop their voices, that they might be heard. Yet there were general students' voices to be heard in the hallways and the classrooms; many were outspoken. But speaking out in class, as it was perjoratively referred to by teachers, falls outside the scheme of the streams. Belligerence was not about to be tolerated at any level in the school, but at the general level, alternative channels for expression were not encouraged. General level English classes treated language manners as a matter of both the curriculum and classroom management, a two-pronged attack on what was ultimately a political question of power and persuasion. The teachers regarded this outspokeness as an occupational hazard of teaching general level classes and not as a possible comment on democratic enfranchisement.

Of course, one might argue at this point, as well as at others in my argument, that the students had brought on themselves this difference in regard by virtue of their attitudes and abilities. But in this case of speaking out, the failure of manners was, on the one hand, a matching of the curriculum's focus on the surface features of language and, on the other, a rudimentary rhetorical ploy intended to influence the teacher. It often worked. But the teacher is still more likely to interpret it as a personal attack rather than as a political statement. The question was whether this outspokeness, and only by a noisy few, or, for that matter, carelessness with capitalisation, demanded the particular differences in the approach to language which marked the streams. The students and teachers both contributed to the unfolding of classroom patterns, both learned from the other in this; yet one does not need to disentangle the web of cause and effect in these responses in order to suggest that an alternative approach is possible. The teachers might have treated speaking out as a rhetoric which arises out of the social resources at hand; they might have considered in a class on language its effectiveness, limitations, and accessibility (I found that the boys were tougher on the girls who spoke out in class than was the teacher). Such could be the first step in a rhetoric for general level classes, a study of being persuasive in a political environment.

It should be clear that language is as often a social, political and moral issue in the English classroom as a literary one. Is there too much here then for the concerned English teacher to handle? Streaming is not about to be dismantled, but the teacher's conception of the streams could stand to be revised. The teacher interested in redressing the imbalance between the streams could begin by conceiving a different future in the language for students in the general level classes, one in which the students might expect to have positions to ably defend, moral and political questions to explore and decide. The teacher, to make this first leap and it is one that will take imagination and verve, will also have to reconceive the matter of language differences and the significance of dialects to which the pamphlet "Students' Right to Their Own Language" serves as an excellent introduction. English teachers have to rid their program in language of popular misconceptions, not about the social importance of the standard to which the students were so attuned, but about its inherent virtues. These attitudes of linguistic superiority do as little to encourage the students' development in language and literacy as the exercises in grammar.

Still this focus on adherence to conventions in standard English most clearly distinguishes the streaming of English classes. As such it tends to exaggerate the differences between students and forms the basis of the moral distinction in the treatment of language in the streams. In light of the only marginal gains in achievement for the better students as a result of streaming, it is a moral distinction which I feel is difficult to defend (Kulik and Kulik 1982). To encourage one level in the fashioning of arguments and the other in adhering to formalities makes a disturbing contribution to the students' education in language, and yet does not seem entirely necessary to the division of classes into streams.

Terri, for example, was one student in the enriched class who spoke openly of the power and the responsibility which she and her classmates had to bear. For her, it had become something of a matter of noblesse oblige:

> All the kids in the enriched classes are well-off. . . . The kids that run the school, like, doing the paper, doing the yearbook, doing everything, like we're all from the same background as the enriched. . . . It's the same people in everything. In the variety show when everyone that's talented gets up, a lot of the black kids are really good with rhythm and dancing and singing and they still don't try out. It's kind of weird. . . . I get mad at them because I think they don't even want to do it, which makes me mad. But they should. . . . And they don't even know what it's about. (Terri, 12Af:40)

She has come to realize, however, a sense of limitations to this knowledge and power. The school may be theirs to run or at least to practice on, but Terri, in running the school newspaper, **The Kipling Times,** had found that propriety, while encouraging discernment, confines power. She stated that the paper was unsupervised by the teachers at the school; she spoke of the "power-rush" such a vehicle might offer, but ultimately:

> There's so much you could do; you could create such a ruckus. . . . It's so stupid—you think if you get a newspaper you can say what you want, but with teachers and the other kids you can't. . . . You have the potential but you can't really use it or you'll get suspended.

The lesson is that these proper forms, these formal powers such as the press, are in their hands, but are also constrained by their responsibility, in a way which desk-top etching will never be. Terri ends up, in her paper, editorializing against the apathetic for not being more involved or interested in extra-curricular activities, the perennial problem for the high school students who run things. She knows more; matters of social class, central to her analysis in the interview, are missing from her paper and so are the teachers she'd like to shake up a bit, though Mr. Allen was Teacher of the Month and Mr. Russell's English as a Second Language program was politely reviewed. Her partial penetration does not disturb her acceptance of the larger determination. She has, ultimately, turned against the victims. But then so did Jane and Ralph; it may be what is required to be, or at least to feel, included. Yet what is not to be overlooked is that in Jane's and Ralph's case it meant a turning against themselves, denying their own voice, in all but its illicit form.

There is another possibility, however, which lies in Terri's experience of language and power. The elements of a more complete understanding are present in Terri's conversation—race, class, power, responsibility—as is the sense of there being a dilemma—"It's kind of weird." Her insight might be furthered by a more realistic and thorough description of the social context of the school and language. It might also contribute to one as well. Terri has begun to perceive the relations of power, propriety and responsibility, but the links are not being explored in her classes (though they are being forged there), nor is she sharing with others how constrained the power-rush really can be and how little her superior language skills have provided. Power is not so much to be had, but is, at least, seen to be had—that is, perhaps, the perk. She has been afforded a grasp of how language works in the social context, and it is lost to the other students. She has, in fact, something more serious to discuss with Jane, Chris and the others who she, in effect, blamed for their marginality, as they have some insight they might share with her about how language and limitation work on another level.

Then, too, Terri has something to share with Annie and Lisa whose concerns with language and power have taken another direction, one which complemented their appearance. Terri has her newspaper; she is pushing out, exploring the range of her voice rather than the regard for her look. She desires to be heard rather than seen. Annie and Lisa's interests in representing themselves at this point are with concessions to propriety in muted but carefully composed tones. They are working on a theory of adequate compensation for inarticulateness. As opposed to the linguistic situation of the majority of black students and of the others at the general level, these female students may imagine the benefits of a deference to a muted role to have their own charm—elegant restaurants and haute couture shops for Lisa and Annie. Their approach to politeness will circumscribe what they can say as well as how it is received (Lakoff 1975).

In this instance, without streaming or standard English at stake, the English program would seem in an excellent position to address the issue of language and women's place. But again the issue is regarded as falling outside the course of an education in language. Throughout this study we have seen that the students and teachers bring to class each day an array of language attitudes and deep-set concerns with their voices. This understanding of language must be explored, rather than ignored, if the English program in the high school is, as we imagine it intends, to expand the students' linguistic universe.

This is only to begin to suggest a direction, and not a program, toward a more honest representation of language in the school. The work of actually developing programs, of lessening the gap between the streams, or of turning language into a greater source of strength, can only grow out of classroom work with teachers and students, rather than emerging, full-blown, from the forehead of studies such as this one.[4] In discussing the results of this study with Mr. Smith, for example, there was a show of interest on his part in exploring matters of language prejudice and power with the students through his Language for Learning work (May 21). It had occurred to him recently that these issues were present in language; how else, he had wondered, could a minority have successfully imposed their language form on so many others.

These students have demonstrated a remarkable sensitivity to the press of both profound and superficial language distinctions, and to the need to meet those crucial moments of linguistic judgement—job interviews, fancy restaurants, meeting people of "high potential." They have fully entered and become a part of the social relations which standard English serves to structure. Yet, as Mr. Allen claimed (June 3), the schools cannot be held solely responsible for the range of attitudes demonstrated by the students; the lessons the students have learned run deeper and are more profound than any that have been intended by the curriculum at Kipling High School. The school has, however, contributed by treating the standard as simply the given, and to the working-up or reification of the concept by the extent of the distinctions the school encourages on the basis of competency with this single form.

The point of any remedial work is principally to assist in Mary's, "we shouldn't put ourselves down"; it is a project for which the English program could do more. If the standard is to be presented as necessary for the world, and the students understand it as nothing less than that, and if Mr. Smith is prepared to promote a policy of "linguistic accuracy," then indeed let an accurate description of the language prevail.[5] De-mystify the "effectiveness" of the standard; deflate the investment of intellectual and moral qualities in its form.

The project speaks to both those who have to avoid putting themselves down, and to those who would put themselves up on such matters as language differences. It is both restorative and critical work. But to restore a fundamental sense of linguistic competence to all speakers, as well as to all language forms, is only the beginning. As Mr. Smith reminded me, the history of the language had been taught in previous years, and he couldn't see that it alone could convince anyone of their own competence (May 21). The point of conviction, however, can only be reached by turning to the students' lives, to the language attitudes they know are dominant and have been, in many cases, realized in themselves. They have an expertise in this; they bring a social text to class which might be critically read and analysed. Paulo Freire's work is, of course, the model for this form of beginning with the students' relationship to the word and the world, and moving towards a more critical awareness through literacy:

> It is a process of knowing with the people how they know things and the level of that knowledge. This means challenging them, through critical reflection, regarding their own practical experience and the ends that motivate them in order, in the end, to organize the findings, and thus replace mere opinions about facts with an increasingly rigorous understanding of their significance. (Freire 1978, p. 25)

The problem is that Brazil and Guinea-Bissau are rather far from Nova Scotia, and one may have trouble imagining the transfer being successfully made. After all, Freire has had his problems getting it to root in his native soil.[6]

In the particular instance of Kipling High School, the students would have to be confronted in both their judgements of others and themselves. It is not just a class—east or west end, academic or general—or a gender issue, but involves individuals doing well or badly by, among other things, the hierarchy of language forms. The whole ineluctable common sense positioning by language must be shaken and realistically described as a cultivated prejudice with a history and a contemporary significance. The standard has not just happened, it must be made clear, as if the cream of language forms has risen to the top, but has required a discourse which sustains this sense of superiority and in which many are participating, some at great personal expense. The very fact that the standard is upheld as appropriate and effective, and that it must be maintained with vigilance, is both its point of strength and susceptability:

> Discourse transmits and produces power; it reinforces it, but it also undermines and exposes it, renders it fragile and makes it possible to thwart. (Foucault 1979, p. 101)

If these discursive practices—which establish the standard as language proper, the male as the generic and dialect as deviation—are distinguished from actual language properties, if the making of the prestige form is unfolded, as an artifice, a political wonder that works through language, then a new economy of language learning and experimentation might be realized.[7] This is not to advocate a utopian pulling out of the linguistic landscape. A revised education in language should not deny the advantage, for instance, which some students bring to school—that, too, is part of the social text—but it can portray the profitable realization of this particular cultural capital as a benefit of an immersion course in a certain form of life, and not an inherent superiority in, for example, language competencies. Nor am I suggesting that English education turn its back on the pursuit of language as an instrument of precision, clarity and insight in the expression of our experience.

A move towards a more realistic description of the significance of language and literature is intended to encourage a re-exploration of language and of the excellent things which can be done with language, to borrow a phrase of Mr. Allen's, by all of the students. The difference I intend is that they will be armed or at least protected against the full appropriation, in what proved to be the students' experience, of clarity and respectability, or in Foucault's terms, of knowledge and power. It is to suggest an English class in which students would not have to lose or risk so much in using language, nor have a basis for taking so much from others. As we have a tongue which would be taught to be well-tempered, we shouldn't flinch from teaching it more honestly, if not more joyously and freely.

Notes

Chapter 1 The Contemporary Setting of Standard English

1. Baugh and Cable (1978) provide an authoritative genealogy for standard English. For a detailed look at the emergence of Chancery English during the reign of Henry V, the first form of English to distinguish itself as a political standard, see Richardson (1980). With regard to the variety of designations, Leitner (1982) cites ten terms current during the early part of this century with "standard English" used first in 1920 by H. Wyld who, interestingly enough, before the first world war preferred the term "well-bred English".

2. Pat Greenfield (1972), for instance, uses Bloomfield's position to construct a cognitive hierarchy, on an international scale for "written" and "oral" languages. For a critique of Greenfield, based on her confounding of literacy and schooling, see Scribner and Cole (1978).

3. This shaping of language can itself, be viewed as a special professional service. It further ensures, as it intended with a well-tempered tongue, that the language, that what can be said, is thoroughly in tune with the profession. These new forms, in all their ostensible adherence to correctness, provide new ways (newspeak) of conceiving experience, enclosing it within the vocabulary of the profession. In education, for example, classroom reflectiveness, daydreaming, and the plain and honest expression of boredom can become "non-attending behaviors," and can be modified accordingly.

4. There are three features which undergo change in popular dialects (Kroch 1978, p. 19): simplified articulation (**and them**: 'n em'), replacement or a loss of perceptually weak segments (**far**: 'fa') and a greater tendency to undergo "natural" vowel shifts (**egg**: 'aig').

5. The question of equality and language differences has kept the literature on education occupied for the last two decades. For a comprehensive survey of this debate see Stubbs (1976) and Edwards (1979), though various aspects of the issue will be raised in this chapter.

6. To gain some idea of how socially responsive this concept of literacy is, consider the National Association for Literacy Advance. A Canadian organization, it has created a constituency for itself by setting the completion of grade nine as necessary for "functional literacy." This in effect gives Nova Scotia an illiteracy level of 20.3%, and Newfoundland, 39.8%. "Television has a lot to do with it," says Bill McGinnis of the Halifax County Literacy Council, though one might suspect otherwise. (Hanton 1981, p. 46). For a more accurate picture of who can read and who is reading in Canada, see Graves and Kinsley (1983), and for a scholarly and historical review of the changing concept of literacy see Resnick and Resnick (1977).

7. Richard Brautigan gives a wonderful sense of a certain disenchantment with literacy in his "Farewell to the First Grade and Hello to the **National Enquirer**": "I let somebody else buy my copy of **The New York Times** instead of me. They could have my copy and responsibility for being a thinking and aware person. I am forty-four years old and thank

God, I got out of the first grade and sometimes all I want to do is have a little mindless fun with the years that are left in my life" (1980, p. 74).

8. A concerned Industrial Relations Commission reported to the American Congress in 1917 on foundations: "The domination of men in whose hands the final control of a large part of America rests is not limited to their employees, but is rapidly extended to control the education and social service of the nation" (cited by Karier 1976, p. 130).

9. They correlate less well with social reality: "The vast preponderance of inequality in schooling, occupational status and earnings has no relationship to differences in measured cognitive ability. A significant fraction of the apparent effect of cognitive ability on educational attainment is spurious. This is true for the apparent effect of ability on occupational status" (Olneck and Crouse 1979, p. 24).

10. On a very selective basis one might consider the critiques of Cicourel et al. (1974) and Gould (1980), against the defences of Jensen (1980) and Herrnstein (1980); though to further complicate matters, or perhaps to reveal what is at stake, there is the case of Cyril Burt (Hearnshaw 1979).

11. The liberal approach to this promise has been one of institutional intervention, though one can never be sure if this is from a belief in the efficacy of the environment or a natural proclivity for institutions—an environment in which liberals, at least, thrive. The conservatives, on the other hand, avoid experiencing responsibility (except of the fiscal sort) or guilt by ascribing differences to genetic history and the "counter-revolution" which has recently reversed the fortunes of these two positions, see Tobin (1981).

12. For an alternative and greatly expanded view of the educational environment as a source of continued inequality see, for example, Bowles and Gintis (1978), Bourdieu and Passeron (1977) or Willis (1977).

13. "There is no doubt that the organic difference which most surely expresses the innate difference in the intellectual scope of individuals of the human species is that of the volume of the brain," wrote Maximilien Parchappe in 1845 (cited by Bisseret 1979, p. 12)

14. Bernstein has commented on his reading of Whorf (1956) in the early and formative years of his work (1971, p. 6).

15. The Sapir—Whorf hypothesis is not to be confused with the German **Weltang-schauung** ("manner of looking at the world") or **Zeitgeist** ("spirit of the period"), which are both reflected in the language and are said to be a product of the times, whether in idealist or materialist terms. These expressions represent interpretations of the world; they are not meant to suggest that the language, in itself, would prevent the realization of certain relationships. The **Weltanschauung** naturalizes some relationships, while making others seem highly improbable but not inaccessable, as would be the case for restricted code users.

16. Bernstein's "progress" in this regard has been reviewed critically by Stubbs (1976, pp. 34-50). More recently Bernstein has, as I mentioned above, redirected his coding concerns to the practices of the school, though his colleagues continue to produce work on language code differences (Holland 1981).

17. See Smith and Lance (1979) for a review of the changed attitudes of English teachers towards dialect over the last decade in response to the work of linguists.

18. My reading of this field owes much to the introductions, reviews, and critiques provided by the English exponents and explorers of the French movement, principally, Coward and Ellis (1977) along with the Centre for Contemporary Cultural Studies group well represented in Hall, Hobson, Lowe and Willis (1980).

Chapter 2   Language in the Streams

1. Howard Becker (1971) has found a similar aversion in the teachers he interviewed to children whose backgrounds were out of line on either side of the middle class milieu of the school. It was an aversion organized around the teacher's strong sense of an "ideal client" and the resulting problems of teaching, discipline and moral acceptability.

2. That teachers, and thus the entire educational bureaucracy, continue to be drawn from the lower middle class has received confirmation in recent studies on an international scale by Schwarzweller and Lyson (1978), as well as by Falk, Falkowski and Lyson (1981).

3. There is one leap in this assumption which perhaps needs justification. Teachers tend to be drawn from a **rural** lower middle class and not New York (Schwarzweller and Lyson 1978). Their general level of anxiety might then be expected to be lower—more pastoral, less anomie. Yet, we might also expect that in upper New York State or in Nova Scotia class distinctions in attitude, such as Labov found, would still hold, though perhaps in a less emphatic manner.

4. This skill, of course, is not restricted to teachers. Light (1979) has found that eight year olds make judgements on the character of people based on whether these people spoke as the students did. It turns out, however, that this is remediable through a short course in sociolinguistics. This approach has also been tried with teachers through in-service programs. A most interesting instance of this is the result of Judge Joiner's decision in **Martin Luther King, Jr. Elementary School Children et al. vs. Ann Arbor School District Board** (1979). The judge ruled that the teachers had failed to be sensitive enough to black English, which thus interfered with the children's right to learn to read. However, the inservice program on black English, which the judge ordered, has not convinced the Ann Arbor officials that such training has improved the teaching of black children (Chambers 1981; "Ann Arbor Results Inconclusive" 1981).

5. "Entrance is **prima facie** evidence that one must be the kind of person the institution was set up to handle. A man in a political prison must be traitorous; a man in a prison must be a law breaker; a man in a mental hospital must be sick, why else would he be there?" (Goffman 1961, p. 84).

6. Actually the "classic" in this field is more often claimed to be Rosenthal and Jacobson's **Pygmalion in the Classroom** (1975), though it tells us considerably less while employing so much more artifice.

7. "He can always seek out other people who think more freely" becomes through this process they term **nominalization** "Seeking out other people with more freedom of thought is always a possibility for him" (Hake and Williams 1981, pp. 435-6).

8. "You see this creature with her kerbstone English: the English that will keep her in the gutter to the end of her days. Well, sir, in three months I could pass that girl off as a duchess at an ambassador's garden party. I could even get her a place as a lady's maid or shop assistant, which requires better English."

9. Felson (1981), for instance, provides a critique of Mead through a more detailed look at self-concept formation in two areas—adolescent concepts of ability and physical attractiveness. He establishes that we do not **uniformly** take on the attitudes of significant others; there are many mitigating factors which lessen this social impact.

10. "Evidence that objective feedback is relied on more than the appraisal of others in making self-evaluations when both are available" is summarized in Felson (1981, p. 70). His own research suggests that institutional judgements—e.g. grades—have more credence than those of significant others.

11. Wilkinson provides a brief but detailed review of this literature (1972, pp. 32-5).

12. James Sledd has found a similarly ambiguous message in the movement for bi-dialectalism in the United States: "No dialect, they keep repeating, is better than any other—yet poor and ignorant children must change theirs unless they want to stay poor and ignorant" (1971, p. 269).

13. For an interesting account of how this process works with a beginning teacher—essentially from a concern with personal inadequacies to a rationalization of failure in terms of pupil inadequacy—see Fuch's "How Teachers Learn to Help Children Fail" (1972).

Chapter 3   Teaching English: Language in the Streams

1. Mr. Avis reported to me that he had earlier that fall convinced Mr.Smith of the implications of prescribing the generic **he**. It is one error, Mr. Smith advised me, that will not be included in the next edition of the **Primer**.

2. The dates of lessons and comments are included to indicate chronological order and documentation in my research notes. Tape recordings were used with two of the teacher interviews (as Mr. Russell and Ms. MacLeod asked not to be taped) and with all of the student interviews, while notes were taken.

3. The "movement," as they point out, is more commonly known, if at all, by the key phrase **Language Across the Curriculum**, which can be traced back to a policy paper prepared by Harold Rosen for the London Association for the Teaching of English (Barnes, Britton, Rosen and L.A.T.E. 1969). It gained considerable impetus in educational systems through the recommendations of the Bullock Report (1975). There has been a recent Nova Scotia Department of Education curriculum guideline, **Language and Learning Across the Curriculum** (1980b) which was adapted from an Ontario Ministry of Education document. Mr. Smith was aware of the Nova Scotia document, but was quite surprised when I informed him of how a similar line and terminology was being used in guidelines prepared by the province for the elementary grades (NSDE 1979; 1980a). There has always been a substantial degree of isolation throughout the curriculum, as well as across it. For a review of these language developments in the teaching of English in England see either Mathieson (1975), Abbs (1981) or Ball (1982).

4. As it tends to be with taxonomies of human behavior, some overlapping exists between categories. The **poetic**, for example, "uses language for its own sake rather than as a means of affecting the world directly." And if that seems unsatisfactory add to it their definition of the **transactional**, from the other end of Britton's continuum which uses "language directly to affect the world by persuading or informing" (p. 2).

5. In presenting their brief to the committee a rivalry emerged between the "Language for Learning" teachers from Kipling and a "cognitive-development" science teacher—a case roughly of Britton vs. Piaget. Mr. Allen, for one, found it riling, particularly as the committee's entire range of curriculum goals had been written within a cognitive framework. The incident illustrated that a scheme of some sort is invaluable for pressing ahead in these professional groups. The schemes would seem to be conveniently aligned with one's discipline—cognitive for the science teacher and language for those in English (though for an ill-fitting Piaget in the service of English, see Bergstrom 1983). It has the result of elevating the clash of interests onto a higher, more theoretical and academic plane.

6. For a rather more precise formulation of how Britton and company became leaders of a "paradigm shift" in the teaching of English in England see Ball (1982, pp. 16-20).

7. The code at the end of a quote identifies a student by grade (10/12), course level (G/A), sex (m/f) and assigned number (1-96).

8. Barthes refers to the connection between language and literature in terms of "the norm of 'accepted' French, a carefully closed language, separated from society by the whole body of the literary myth, a consecrated mode of writing . . . a tabernacle of the awe inspiring mystery: French Literature" (Barthes 1968, pp. 59-60).

9. I quickly became so absorbed in the lesson that I failed to record the richness of references to Renaissance sources and beliefs, the student insights, and the learning that emerged between the first reading at the beginning of the class and what at least I felt on the final reading. For a moment I forgot where I was—it was a lesson out of school.

10. This "ability to make their language useful" generally characterizes the distinction literate people would make for themselves. The fact is (a) that we would have no language resources that weren't in some sense "useful" to us and (b) that everyone has **just** that ability to make their language "useful," or it would not have developed. The characterization actually refers to the specific use of language as a means of succeeding in specific locations, for example, a school. It has, however, proved convenient to generalize in such a fashion when writing of the language abilities of the "illiterate."

11. "Up to half marks off" is, according to Mr.Smith, departmental policy for examinations (February 15). It was brought to my attention by a student in 12G; the one student I asked about it in 12A said she didn't think marks were being taken off in her class for spelling errors (12Af:34), which Mr.Allen later confirmed (May 12).

12. Frank Smith has recently written on this dichotomy between mechanical and intellectual concerns in writing. He treats them as essentially incompatible as a focus of attention; if one is perceived as the primary basis of evaluation it will absorb what attention there is in the writing (1982, pp. 23-4). This can be countered by revising and editing, but in an environment of assignment and examination writing that would require a rather special dedication.

13. What did come up were lessons on vocabulary (Nov. 18), capitalization (Dec. 1, 2), and grammar (Jan. 12; Feb. 15, 17).

14. Hargreaves' study of social relations in a streamed secondary school documented the teaching practice in mathematics of going back to the basics to the point of retarding progress through sheer boredom—"We'd have done harder work better," as one lad put it. This was "based on the correct assumption that most of the pupils in 3D [lower stream] were far from expert at the theory or practice of simple mathematical calculations" (Hargreaves 1971, pp. 203-4).

15. Numbered statements refer to items on the Sentence Completion Test (see table 1, chapter 4) which I designed for this study on attitudes toward language, literacy and schooling. The students were provided with 40 stubs and asked to complete them; the dash is used to separate stub from student response. For a complete analysis of the results see the following two chapters.

16. Hargreaves noted in his study a similar pattern of assignment, which does not go unnoticed by the students nor the teachers (1971, pp. 201-2).

17. The recognition of a male dominance, in this instance of language and the classroom, is an example of an exclusion of females from the power struggle in the class. It is a constructing of women's silence and the establishing of the dominant and the muted, part of which is discussed above in chapter two of this study (Spender 1981). Clarricoates has also found in her research that "girls do accept the superior status of boys"; as "their confidence is being undermined": in class they have "learned to accept that the male figure is all important

and speaks with the voice of authority" (1981, p. 197).

18. In my sample of 96 students from the four English classes, there were twelve black students of whom only one was in an advanced English course.

19. To provide an instance of how this prejudice can gel I offer these candid remarks from a student-teacher who happened to be "practice teaching" John Hersey's **Hiroshima** to a general level class across the hall from Mr.Russell's room: "I felt great contempt for them [the three male black students]. Surely they of all people would know what it must be like to be made fun of and ridiculed unfairly. Here they were laughing at horribly maimed people. I was angry at their complete shallowness and stupidity. I told them that they were very immature and they had a lot of growing up to do. I should have saved my breath" (Campbell 1982, p. 15).

20. For a recent analysis of the greater disproportion of black suspensions and expulsions in American schools see Bennett and Harris (1982). They have found that they causes still are "related to an overall orientation of White predominance which includes individual and institutional racisim" (p. 420).

Chapter 4   Learning English: The Way the Queen Talks

1. Unless otherwise indicated the use of the term, "statistically significant," in this study refers to a .05 level of confidence.

2. For instance, one interesting area which, however, proved not to be directly related to language was the tendency of grade 12 students to be more cynical about schooling— significantly more negative on what schooling can provide (item 11); and significantly more likely to see contradictions in the school (item 9). These and other results will be retained possibly for a future analysis on the students' more generalized response to the school.

3. In a detailed study of women writers of the last century, Gilbert and Gubar have explored a common and distinctively female literary tradition which reflects a profound and anxious struggle against a patriarchial field. Working under Harold Bloom's "anxiety of influence" thesis, they provide an analysis of the extra psychological effort it took for women to begin to write in the literary tradition: "Unlike her male counterpart, then, the female artist must first struggle against the effects of a socialization which makes conflict with the will of her (male) precursors seem inexpressively absurd, futile, or even—as in the case of the Queen in "Little Snow White"—self annihilating. . . . Her battle, however, is not against her (male) precursors reading of the world but against his reading of **her**" (1979, p. 49, original emphasis).

4. Names have been assigned and used in this chapter with the eight students whose comments are dealt with on an individual basis in chapter five.

5. For a discussion of the innaccessability of reading skills for direct evaluation, as it affects both teacher assessment and the meaning of literacy in the classroom see Heap (1980) and, in response, Willinsky (1981).

6. Dale Spender, while taking issue with some of the research in this area, has pointed out that the greater concern with "politeness" which has been found in female speech can be interpreted as a response to the subservient position expected of women (1979, pp. 36-8). It would seem that civility is a social role for women which will be comfortably entertained by men, while effectively circumscribing what women can possibly say or do.

7. This really calls for a footnote on the colonial setting of this school situated in a town which was still accused on occasion of having a "garrison mentality." Mr. Smith was indeed a

British expatriate who regularly began his classes, not with "God Save the Queen," though as I say she did come up with regularity, but often with critical acclaim for, and exhortations to watch, British television productions—"Brideshead Revisited," "Life on Earth" (November 10, 17; January 5, 12, 19; February 2). There were references indicating that Britain was the mother country of our mother tongue on a number of the SCT's (19% of Mr. Smith's 10A; 7% of the entire sample). Britain might serve to provide a kind of geographical distancing or elevation, to supplement the class one, for the concept of a standard language.

8. The greater facility with which we believe young children acquire a second language has recently been challenged by research demonstrating that "older students are better than younger ones in learning syntax, vocabulary and the structure of language" (Matas 1982, p. 2). This undermining of a theory of developmental receptiveness in language learning places a greater emphasis on social factors such as attitudes and identity.

9. There is also support to be found for this in the research reported in Spender and Sarah (1980), though the distinction of academic levels is not made. Parker (1973) has found, in a similar vein, that both male and female students regarded classroom talk, particularly questioning and challenging, as a "masculine behavior" (reported in Clarricoated, 1981, p. 196).

10. Just to give some sense of how this greater sense of male domination among general level students might be explored, one could consider the differences between popular fiction and the "literature" to which the general and academic students, respectively, are exposed both in and out of the schools. The English Studies Group associated with the University of Birmingham, for example, has found in their critical examination of one popular form, the romance, "the silencing subjection of the woman and the accompanying closure of narrative codes; the exclusion of irony in the rigorous simplification of the narrative "grammar"; the prominence of a sententious vein of common sense" (The English Studies Group 1980, p. 261). It does suggest that the forms are, as they conclude, "far from ideologically inert," and might well provide some insight into the sources of these lessons learned.

11. "But the study of literature has traditionally been felt to have a unique effectiveness in opening the mind and illuminating it, purging the mind of prejudices and received ideas, in making the mind free and active" (Trilling 1965, p. 4).

Chapter 5 The Significance of Standard English: Eight Students

1. Official explanations from the Nova Scotia Department of Education suggest that the general level is for those "who are not suited for nor interested in intensive preparation for higher education" and are of "average intelligence" (Moffat 1961). Teachers in the province have indicated that they find general level students to be distinguished by a certain lack of motivation, initiative, industry, self-discipline, attention span and as well need greater reinforcement (Macdonald 1981, pp. 38-40).

2. I suspect that this is a defence against the racial designations made, though quietly, by the other students and the teachers. What was absent from Ralph's comments, and from those of the other black students, was a sense of language differences as a point of identity, as a form of their own affirmation against exclusion. For a study of language used by black teenagers as a strong point of cultural pride and social solidarity, see Folb (1980).

3. "It was a small town in those days and a child revealed everything about himself, as it were, from the way he nosed his bicycle out of the stands in front of the school. Each cardinal direction indicated who and what you were, what your father did, and what your

prospects (in life) were going to be" (from a short story by Clark Blaise 1982, p. 20).

4. Chris' views of the east enders did receive corroboration from within their ranks: "10. Middle class talk—is unreal, all abstracts, no reality to base views on. We have the silver spoon in our mouth" (12Af:50).

5. Eleanor Macdonald reports that in Nova Scotia a climb to the academic level from the general was "rare." The student had to, in most cases, repeat the year over again at the academic level (Macdonald 1981, pp. 54-5).

6. "In every culture education aims to develop individuals whose sensitivities and whose anxieties will be useful and reassuring to the kind of people who already wield power" (Friedenberg 1959, p. 74).

Chapter 6   The Conclusion: The Well-Tempered Tongue

1. While immediately apparent to anyone sitting in a classroom or talking to the students, this challenge has been seriously overlooked by much of the critical educational theory; corrective measures are to be found, for example, in Corrigan and Willis (1980) with their attack on the overdeterminations of discourse theory, and Giroux (1981) for his dislodging of the school as the central determining force in critical theory.

2. Jean Anyon has similarly found in her study of elementary classrooms that "these types of resistance to degrading work involved, then, attempts to ease the situation through language and other defensive actions—but without changing the power relations or making fundamental demands" (1981, p. 122). The difference between what we have found is between students "easing" out of work, and students attempting to save face and something more besides.

3. Yet what is also lost sight of in this presentation are the ways in which "the rules" and the dictates of decorum can as easily and intentionally obscure, if not obstruct, the truth. It is the other power of language, and a most public and statesman-like one at that.

4. This is not to say it cannot be attempted. Anyon, for one, has recently advanced a program for "enriched" students (as well as one for those who are not) "using penetrative consciousness," "politicizing cultural resistance" and "developing counter ideologies." She intends by this work "to engender a bit of guilt" while pointing out to these students that they "are in an excellent position to provide leadership in movements for social change and that, as such, they would gain in **power** from attempts to dislodge the present capitalist class" (1981, p. 128-9, original emphasis).

5. As James Sledd has noted with some bite on these practical considerations of job-prep: "we should be hard-headedly consistent in our brutalities and try to eradicate the vices which do enrage employers—like intellectual questioning, or the suspicion that ours is not the best of all possible worlds" (1971, p. 277).

6. Freire's work has, however, made it as far north as New York where little in commitment, at least, has been lost. Ira Shor (1980) has turned Freire's **conscientizacaon** into "liberatory education" and adapted it to the new environs: "A critical classroom pushes against the conditioned boundaries of consciousness" (p. 93). What this means, briefly, are some not uncommon teaching techniques—timed uninterrupted writing, for example—and topics—"my worst teacher." But beyond being practical, Shor pushes towards what is essentially a course in self-construction and self-defence through literacy—as assertion— and a realization of a certain commoness of experience—towards solidarity and organization (pp. 125-55). It lacks the organic integrity suggested by Freire's "generative words" out of

which emerge the relations of language, work and culture. But it does use and challenge these relations in the students' lives; it does demonstrate the possibilities in the context of urban America, community colleges and open admissions.

7. On a theoretical level, an initial objective could be to examine how the distinctions have been established and, in particular, how the norm is maintained, against which all else is defined as deviation. Black and Coward, in their critique of Spender's work (1980), see this as the very starting point for exploring sexism. It is also their point that the dominance is not in the language—in the syntax or the semantics—but arises out of what they term, after Foucault, discursive practices: "We see one of the major political problems confronting feminism to be the need to force men to recognize themselves as **men**. The discursive formation which allows men to represent themselves as non-gendered and to define women constantly according to their sexual status is a discursive formation with very definite effects" (Black and Coward 1981, p. 81).

References

Abbs, Peter. **English for Diversity: A Polemic.** London: Heinemann, 1969.

"Ann Arbor Results Inconclusive." **Educational Leadership.** 38, 6 (March 1981), 476.

Anyon, Jean. "Elementary Schooling and Distinctions of Social Class." **Interchange**, 12, 2-3 (1981), p. 118-32.

----------. "Reproduction, Contestation, and Curriculum: An Essay in Self-Criticism." **Interchange**, 12, 2-3 (1981), 27-47.

Balibar, Etienne and Macherey, Pierre. "On Literature as an Ideological Form." In Robert Young (ed.), **Untying the Text: A Post-Structuralist Reader**. London: Routledge and Kegan Paul, 1981, pp. 79-99.

Balibar, Renee. **Les Francais Fictifs.** Paris: Hachette, 1974.

Ball, Stephen J. "Competition and Conflict in the Teaching of English: a Socio-Historical Analysis." **Journal of Curriculum Studies,** 14 (1982), 1-28.

Barnes, D., Britton, J., Rosen, H. and L.A.T.E. **Language, the Learner and the School.** Hammondsworth: Penguin, 1969.

Baron, Dennis E. **Grammar and Good Taste: Reforming the American Langauge.** New Haven: Yale, 1982.

Barthes, Roland. **Writing Degree Zero**. Boston: Beacon, 1968.

Baugh, Albert C. and Cable, Thomas. **A History of the English Language.** 3rd ed. Englewood Cliffs, N.J.: Prentice-Hall, 1978.

Becker, Howard S. "Social Class Variations in the Teacher-Pupil Relationship." In B. R. Cosin et al. (eds.), **School and Society: A Sociological Reader.** 2nd ed. London: Routlege and Kegan Paul, 1971, pp. 119-125.

Bennet, Christine, and Harris, J. John III. "Suspensions and Expulsions of Male and Black Students: A Study of the Causes of Disproportionality." **Urban Education**, 16, 4 (January 1982), 399-425.

Bereiter, Carl and Englemann, S. **Teaching Disadvantaged Children in the Pre-School.** Englewood Cliffs, N.J.: Prentice Hall, 1966.

Berger, Peter, and Luckmann, Thomas. **The Social Construction of Reality: A Treatise on the Sociology of Knowledge**. New York Doubleday, 1966.

Bergstrom, Robert. "Discovery of Meaning: Development of Formal Thought in the Teaching of Literature." **College English**, 45, 8 (December 1983), 745-55.

Bernstein, Basil. **Class, Codes and Control; Theoretical Studies Towards a Sociology of Language**. Vol. I. London: Routledge and Kegan Paul, 1971.

----------, (ed.) **Class, Codes and Control: Applied Studies Towards a Sociology of Language**. Vol. II. London: Routledge and Kegan Paul, 1973.

----------. **Class, Codes and Control: Towards a Theory of Educational Transmission.** Vol. III. London: Routledge and Kegan Paul, 1977.

----------. "Codes, Modalities, and the Process of Cultural Reproduction: A Model." **Language in Society,** 10 (1981), 327-63.

Bettleheim, Bruno and Zelan, Karen. **On Learning to Read.** New York: Knopf, 1982.

Bisseret, Noelle. **Education, Class Language and Ideology.** London: Routledge and Kegan Paul, 1979.

Black, Maria and Coward, Rosalind. "Linguistic, Social and Sexual Relations: A Review of Dale Spender's **Man Made Language.**" **Screen Education,** 38 (1981), 69-75.

Blaise, Clark. "South." **Canadian Forum,** 62, 718 (May 1982), 19-20, 37.

Bloomfield, Leopold. "Literate and Illiterate Speech." **American Speech,** 2 (1927), 432-9.

Botstein, Leon. "Imitative Literacy." **Partisan Review,** 48, 3 (1981), 399-408.

Bourdieu, Pierre. "The School as a Conservative Force." In John Eggleston (ed.), **Contemporary Research in the Sociology of Education.** London: Methuen, 1974, pp. 32-46.

Bourdieu, Pierre and Passeron, J. C. **Reproduction in Education, Society and Culture.** Trans. R. Nice. London: Sage, 1977.

----------. **The Inheritors.** Chicago: University of Chicago Press, 1979.

Bowles, S. and Gintis, H. **Schooling in Capitalist America.** New York: Basic, 1977.

Brautigan, Richard. **The Tokyo-Montana Express.** New York: Delacorte, 1980.

Britton, James. **Language and Learning.** Hammondsworth: Penguin, 1972.

Brook, G. L. **The Varieties of English.** London: Macmillan, 1973.

Bullock, Allan. **A Language For Life.** London: HMOS, 1975.

Butler, William. **The Butterfly Revolution.** New York: Ballentine, 1979.

Campbell, Duain. "Socialization: a Student Teacher and Black Students." Unpublished paper, Dalhousie University, 1982.

Castellan, N. J. "On the Partitioning of Contingency Tables." **Psychological Bulletin,** 64 (1965), 330-38.

Cazden, C. B. "Language Programs for Young Children, Notes from England and Wales." In C. S. Laratelli (ed.), **Language Training in Early Childhood.** Urbana, Ill.: University of Illinois Press, 1971, pp. 18-53.

Chambers. John W. "Black English: A Response." **Educational Leadership,** 38, 6 (March 1981), 477.

Cicourel, Aaron et al. **Language Use and School Performance.** New York: Academic Press, 1974.

Clairmount, Donald and Magill, Dennis. **Nova Scotia Blacks: An Historical and Structural Overview.** Halifax, N.S.: Institute of Public Affairs, Dalhousie University, 1970.

Clarricoates, Katherine. "The Experience of Patriarchial Schooling." **Interchange,** 12, 2-3 (1981), pp. 185-205.

Conference on College Composition and Communication. "Students' Right to Their Own Language." **College Composition and Communication,** 25 (Fall 1974), 1-32.

Corrigan, Philip and Willis, Paul. "Cultural Forms and Class Mediations." **Media, Culture and Society,** 2 (1980), 297-312.

Coward, R. And Ellis, J. **Language and Materialism: Developments in Semiology and the Theory of the Subject.** London: Routledge and Kegan Paul, 1977.

Currie, Ian. "The Sapir-Whorf Hypothesis." In Jane Curtis and John Petras (eds.), **The Sociology of Knowledge: A Reader.** New York: Praeger, 1970, pp. 403-21.

Dennison, George. **Lives of Children: The Story of First Street School**. New York: Random House, 1969.

Duckworth, Eleanor. "Language and Thought." In Milton Schwebel and Jane Ralph (eds.), **Piaget in the Classroom**. New York: Basic Books, 1973, pp. 132-54.

----------. "Either We're Too Early and They Can't Learn It or We're Too Late and They Know It Already." **Harvard Educational Review**, 49 (1979), pp. 297-312.

Edwards, John. **Language and Disadvantage**. Amsterdam: Elsivier, 1979.

The English Studies Group, 1978-1979. "Recent Developments in English Studies at the Centre." In **Culture, Media, Language**. London: Hutchinson, 1980, pp. 235-68.

Falk, William, Falkowski, Carolyn and Lyson, Thomas A. " 'Some Plans to Become Teachers: Further Elaboration and Specification." **Sociology of Education**, 54 (1981), 64-69.

Faure, Alain and Ranciere, Jacques. **La Parole Ouviere, 1830-1851**. Paris: Union generale d'edition, 1976.

Felson, R. B. "Social Sources of Information in the Development of Self." **Sociological Quarterly**, 22, 1 (1981), 69-80.

Fender, Robert, and Lambert, Wallace. "Speech Style and Scholastic Success: the Tentative Relationships and the Possible Implications for Lower Social Class Children." In Roger Shuy (ed.), **Report of the Twenty-Third Annual Round Table Meeting On Linguistics and Language Studies**. Washington, D.C.: Georgetown University Press, 1973, pp. 237-71.

Folb, Edith. **Runnin' Down Some Lines: The Language and Culture of Black Teenagers**. Cambridge Mass.: Harvard University Press, 1980.

Foucault, Michel. **The Archeology of Knowledge and the Discourse on Language**. New York: Harper and Row, 1972.

----------. **The History of Sexuality**. Vol. I: An Introduction. Trans. Robert Hurley. London: Allen Lane, 1979.

----------. **Power/Knowledge: Selected Interviews and Other Writings, 1972-1977**. Ed. C. Gordon. New York: Pantheon, 1980.

Fraser, Ian. **Like Language**. Toronto: Language Associates, 1976.

Freire, Paulo. **Pedagogy in Process: Letters to Guinea-Bissau**. New York: Seabury Press, 1978.

Friedenberg, Edgar Z. **The Vanishing Adolescent**. New York: Dell, 1959.

----------. **Coming of Age in America**. New York: Random House, 1965a.

----------. "Truth: Upper, Middle and Lower." In his **The Dignity of Youth and Other Atavisms**. Boston: Beacon Press, 1965b.

Fuchs, Estelle. "How Teachers Learn to Help Children Fail." In Nell Keddie (ed.), **Tinker, Tailor: The Myth of Cultural Deprivation**. Hammondsworth: Penguin, 1973, pp. 75-85.

Gidney, R. D. "Elementary Education in Upper Canada: A Reassessment." In M. B. Katz and P. H. Mattingly (eds.), **Education and Social Change: Themes from Ontario's Past**. New York: New York University Press, 1975, pp. 3-27.

Gilbert, S. and Gubar, S. **The Madwoman in the Attic: the Woman Writer and the Nineteenth Century Literary Imagination**. New Haven, Conn.: Yale University Press, 1979

Giroux, Henry A. "Hegemony, Resistance and the Paradox the Educational Reform." **Interchange**, 12, 2-3 (1981), 3-26.

Goffman, Erving. **The Presentation of Self in Everyday Life**. New York: Doubleday, 1959.

----------. **Asylum**. New York: Doubleday, 1961.

Gold, Joseph, (ed.). **In the Name of Language!** Toronto: Macmillan, 1975.

Gould, Stephen Jay. "Jensen's Last Stand." **New York Review of Books**, 27 (May 1, 1980), 38-44.

Graff, Harvey. **The Literacy Myth: Literacy and Social Structure in the Nineteenth Century City**. New York: Academic Press, 1979.

Grant, George. "Literature and the Uncertainty of Modern Criticism." **The Globe and Mail**, 7 May 1983, p. E18.

Graves, Frank and Kinsley, Brian. "Elective Illiteracy in Canada." **Canadian Journal of Education**, 8, 4 (Fall 1983), 315-31.

Greenfield, Pat. "Oral and Written Language: The Consequences for Cognitive Development in Africa, the United States, and England." **Language and Speech**, 15 (1972), 169-78.

Hacker, Andrew. "Creating American Inequality." **New York Review of Books**, 27, 4 (March 20, 1980), 27.

Hake, Rosemary, and Williams, John. "Style and Its Consequences: Do as I Do, Not as I Say." **College English**, 43, 5 (September 1981), 433-51.

Hall, S., Hobson, D., Lowe, A. and Willis, P. (eds.). **Culture, Media and Language: Working Papers in Cultural Studies, 1972-79**. London: Hutchinson in association with the Centre for Contemporary Cultural Studies; University of Birmingham, 1980.

Halliday, M. A. K. "Introduction." In Basil Bernstein (ed.), **Class, Codes and Control: Applied Studies Toward a Sociology of Language**. Vol. II. London: Routledge and Kegan Paul, 1973.

Halsey, A. M., Heath, A. F. and Ridge, J. M. **Origins and Destinations: Family, Class and Education in Modern Britain**. Oxford: Clarendon Press, 1980.

Hanton, Elizabeth. "Johnny's Grown Up. Shouldn't He Know His ABC's?" **Atlantic Insight**, August/September 1981, pp. 46-9.

Hargreaves, David. "Teacher-Pupil Relations in a Streamed Secondary School." In A. Morrison and K. McIntyre. Hammondsworth: Penguin, 1972, pp. 198-212.

Heap, James. "What Counts as Reading: Limits to Certainty in Assessment." **Curriculum Inquiry**, 10, 3 (1980), pp. 265-92.

Hearnshaw, Leslie S. **Cyril Burt, Psychologist**. Ithaca, N.Y.: Cornell University Press, 1979.

Heathcote, Dorothy. "From Particular to the Universal". In D. Robinson (ed.), **Exploring Theatre and Education**. London Heinemann, 1980.

Henderson, Jim and Shepard, Ronald. **Language Matters**. Don Mills, Ontario: Nelson, 1975.

Herrnstein, R. J. "In Defence of Intelligence Tests." **Commentary**, 69, 2 (February 1980), 40-51.

Hinton, S. E. **The Outsiders**. New York: Dell, 1967.

----------. **That Was Then, This Is Now**. New York: Dell, 1971.

Holland, Jane. "Social Class and Changes in Orientation to Meaning." **Sociology**, 15, 1 (February 1981), 1-18.

Humbolt. W. von. **Linguistic Variability and Intellectual Development**. Trans. G. C. Buck and F. A. Raven. Philadelphia: University of Pennsylvania Press, 1971.

Husen, Torsten. **The School in Question: A Comparative Study of the School and Its Future in Western Society**. Oxford: Oxford University Press, 1979.

Jackendoff, Ray. "Grammar as Evidence for Conceptual Structure." In Morris Halle et al. (eds.), **Linguistic Theory and Psychological Reality**. Cambridge Mass.: MIT, 1978, pp. 201-28.

Jensen, Arthur. **Bias in Mental Testing**. New York: Free Press, 1980.

Johnson, Richard. "Notes on the Schooling of the English Working Class, 1780-1850." In R. Dale et al. (eds.), **Schooling and Capitalism: A Sociological Reader**. London: Routledge and Keagan Paul, 1976, pp. 44-54.

Jones, Richard Foster. **The Triumph of the English Language**. Stanford: Stanford University Press, 1953.

Kahane, Henry and Kahane, Renee. "Decline and Survival of Western Prestige Languages." **Language**, 55, 1 (1979), 183-99.

Karier, Clarence J. "Testing for Order and Control in the Corporate Liberal State." In Roger Dale et al, (eds.), **Schooling and Capitalism: A Sociological Reader**. London: Routledge and Kegan Paul, 1976, pp. 128-40.

Kelly, Thomas P. **The Black Donnellys: The True Story of Canada's Most Barbaric Feud**. Toronto: Modern Canadian Library, 1974.

Kinneavy, James. "Restoring the Humanities: The Return of Rhetoric from Exile." In James Murphy (ed.), **The Rhetorical Tradition and Modern Writing**. New York: Modern Language Association of America, 1982,

Kroch, Anthony S. "Toward a Theory of Social Dialect Variation." **Language in Society**, 7 (1978), 17-36.

Kulik, C. and Kulik, J. "Effects of Ability Grouping on Secondary School Students: A Meta-Analysis of Evaluation Findings." **American Educational Research Journal**, 19 (Fall 1982), 415-428.

Illich, Ivan. "Vernacular Values and Education." **Teachers College Record**, 81, 1 (1979), 31-76.

Innis, Harold. **The Bias of Communication**. Toronto: University of Toronto Press, 1951.

Labov, William. "Hypercorrection in the Lower Middle Class as a Factor of Linguistic Change." In his **Sociolinguistic Patterns**. Philadelphia: University of Pennsylvania, 1972a, pp. 122-42.

----------. **Language in the Inner City**. Philadelphia: University of Pennsylvania, 1972b.

----------. "The Logic of Nonstandard English." In Nell Keddie (ed.), **Tinker, Tailor: The Myth of Cultural Deprivation**. Hammondsworth: Penguin, 1973, pp. 21-66.

Lakoff, Robin. **Language and Woman's Place**. New York: Harper, 1975.

Leavis, F. R. **The Living Principle: English as a Discipline of Thought**. New York: Oxford University Press, 1975.

Leitner, Gerhard. "The Consolidation of 'Educated Southern English' as a Model in the Early 20th Century." **IRAL** 20, 2 (May 1982), 91-107.

Leonard, Sterling. **The Doctrine of Correctness in English Usage: 1700-1800**. 1929; rpt. New York: Russell and Russell, 1962.

----------. **Current English Usage**. Chicago: NCTE Monograph, 1932.

----------. **The Savage Mind**. Chicago: University of Chicago Press, 1966.

Levi-Strauss, Claude. **The Savage Mind**. Chicago: University of Chicago Press, 1966.

Levine, Kenneth. "Functional Literacy: Fond Illusions and False Economies." **Harvard Educational Review**, 52 (August 1982), 249-266.

Lewis, M. M. **Language, Thought and Personality in Infancy and Childhood**. London: Harrp, 1963.

Light, R. L. "Children's Linguistic Attitudes: A Study and Some Implications." **Language Arts**, 56 (February 1979), 132-9.

Luria, A. R. and Yudovich, F. Ia. **Speech and the Development of Mental Processes in the Child**. Introduction By James Britton. Hammondsworth: Penguin, 1971.

Lyman, R. L. **Summary of Investigations Relating to Grammar, Language and Composition**. Chicago: University of Chicago Press, 1929.

Macaulay, R. K. S. **Language, Social Class, and Education: A Glassgow Study**. Edinburgh: Edinburgh University Press, 1977.

Macdonald, Eleanor. **General Courses, High School Leaving Courses, Non-College Bound Courses: The Teachers' Viewpoints**. Halifax: Atlantic Institute of Education, 1981.

Macnamara, John. "Attitudes and Learning a Second Language." In R. Shuy and R. Fasols (eds.), **Language Attitudes: Current Trends and Prospects**. Washington, D.C.: Georgetown University Press, 1973, pp. 36-40.

Marckwardt, Albert and Walcott, Fred. **Facts about Current English**. New York: Appleton-Century, 1938.

Mare, Robert D. "Change and Stability in Educational Stratification." **American Sociological Review**, 46, 1 (February 1981), 72-87.

Martell, George. "The Politics of Reading and Writing." In R. Dale et al. (eds.), **Schooling and Capitalism**. London: Routledge and Kegan Paul, 1976, pp. 105-9.

Matas, Robert. "Convention Challenged: Youth Has No Special Advantage in Learning Languages, Report Says." **The Globe and Mail**, 16 April, 1982, pp. 1-2.

Mathieson, Margaret. **The Preachers of Culture: A Study of English and Its Teachers**. London: George Allen and Unwin, 1975.

McConnell, R. E. **Our Own Voice: Canadian English and How It Is Studied**. Toronto: Gage, 1979.

McMaster. R. J. **Communicating in Your World**. Don Mills, Ontario: Academic Press, 1979.

Mead, George H. "The Problem of Society: How We Become Ourselves." In his **On Social Psychology: Selected Papers**. Ed. Anslem Strauss. Chicago: University of Chicago Press, 1956, pp. 19-42.

----------. **Selected Writings**. Ed. A. J. Reck. Indianappolis: Bobbs Merrill, 1964.

Mowat, Farley. **Two Against the North**. Toronto: Scholastic, 1977.

Myers, L. M. **The Roots of Modern English**. Boston: Little, Brown, 1966.

Nabokov, Vladimir. **Lectures on Literature**. Ed. Fred Bowers. Introd. John Updike. London: Weidenfeld and Nicholson, 1980.

Nova Scotia Department of Education (NSDE). **Aspects of English: Junior High School, A Guide to English Language Study**. Halifax, 1972.

----------. **The Novel in Senior High School**. Halifax, 1974.

----------. **Learning about Language in the Elementary School**. Halifax, 1978.

----------. **Writing in the Elementary School**. Halifax, 1979.

----------. **Elementary Language Arts: An Overview**. Halifax, 1980a.

----------. **Language and Learning Across the Curriculum: Secondary English 7-10**. Halifax, 1980b.

Olneck, Michael R. and Crouse, James. "The IQ Meritocracy Reconsidered: Cognitive Skills and Adult Success in United States." **American Journal of Education**, 88, 1 (November 1979), 1-32.

Parker, A. **Sex Differences in Classroom Intellectual Argumentation**. Unpublished M.Sc. Thesis, Pennsylvania State University, 1973.

Payne, Jame S. et al. **Head Start: A Tragicomedy With Epilogue**. New York: Behavioral Publications, 1973.

Penner, Philip and McConnell, Ruth. **Language Learning**. (A Revision of **Learning English**.) Toronto: MacMillan, 1977.

Piaget, Jean. **Six Psychological Studies**. Trans. A. Tenzer. London: University of London Press, 1968.

Resnick, Daniel and Resnick, Lauren B. "The Nature of Literacy: an Historical Explanation." **Harvard Educational Review**, 43, 3 (August 1977), 370-84.

Richardson, Malcolm. "Henry V, the English Chancery, and Chancery English." **Speculum**, 55, 4 (Octover 1980), 726-50.

Rist, Ray. "Student Social Class and Teacher Expectations: the Self-Fulfilling Prophecy in Ghetto Eduation." **Harvard Educational Review**, 40 (1970), 411-51.

Rogers, Sinclair. "The Language of Children and Adolescents and the Language of Schooling." In Sinclair Rogers (ed.), **They Don't Speak Our Language: Essays on the Language World of Children and Adolescents**. London: Edward Arnold, 1976, pp. 13-33.

Rosen, Harold. **Language and Class: A Critical Look at the Theories of Basil Bernstein**. Bristol: Falling Water Press, 1972.

Rosenberg, M. **Society and Adolescent Self-Image**. Princeton, N.J.: Princeton University Press, 1965.

Rosenthal, Robert and Jacobson, Lenore. **Pygmalion in the Classroom**. New York: Holt, Rinehart and Winston, 1966.

Ross, Alan. "U and Non-U: An Essay in Sociological Linguistics." In Nancy Mitford (ed.), **Noblesse Oblige**. London: Hammish Hamilton, 1956.

Schwartz, Judy. "Dialect and Learning to Read." In Judy Schwartz (ed.), **Teaching the Linguistically Diverse**. Rochester: The New York State English Teachers Council, 1980, pp. 47-59.

Schwarzeller, Harry K. and Lyson, Thomas A "Some Plans to Become Teachers: Determinants of Career Specification among Rural Youth in Norway, Germany and the United States." **Sociology of Education**, 51 (January 1978), 29-43.

Scribner, Sylvia and Cole, Michael. "Literacy Without Schooling: Testing for Intellectual Effects." **Harvard Educational Review**, 48, 4 (November 1978), 448-61.

----------. **The Psychology of Literacy**. Cambridge, Mass.: Harvard University Press, 1981.

Searle, Chris. **The Forsaken Lover: White Words and Black People.** Hammondsworth: Penguin, 1972.

Seligman, C. R., Tucker, G. R. and Lambert, W. E. "The Effects of Speech Style and Other Attributes on Teachers' Attitudes Towards Pupils." **Language in Society**, 1 (1972), 131-42.

Sennett, Richard and Cobb, Jonathan. **The Hidden Injuries of Class**. New York: Vintage, 1972.

Seppanen, Aimo. "On the Notion of Correct Usage." **Modern Sprak**, 75, 3 (1981), 225-33.

Shor, Ira. **Critical Teaching and Everyday Life**. Montreal: Black Rose Press, 1980.

Sidney, Philip. **An Apology for Poetry**. 1595; rpt. Ed. F. Robinson. New York: Bobbs-Merrill, 1970.

Simon, John. **Paradigms Lost: Reflections On Literacy and Its Decline**. New York: Potter, 1980.

Sledd, James. "Bidialectism: The Linguistics of White Supremacy." In Arthur Daigon and Ronald Laconte (eds.), **Challenge and Change in the Teaching of English**. Boston: Allyn and Bacon, 1971, pp. 265-78.

----------. "In defense of the **Students' Right**." College English, 45 (November 1983), 667-675.

Smith, Frank. **Writing and the Writer**. New York: Holt, Rinehart and Wintson, 1982.

Smith, Riley, B. and Lance, Donald M. "Standard and Disparate Varieties of English in the United States: Educational and Sociopolitical Implications." **International Journal of the Sociology of Language**, 21, (1979), 127-40.

Spender, Dale. **Man Made Language**. London: Routledge and Kegan Paul, 1980.

Spender, Dale and Sarah, Elizabeth. **Learning to Lose**. London: Women's Press, 1980.

Stubbs, Michael. **Language, Schools and Classrooms**. London: Methuen, 1976.

Symonds, P. M. "Practice vs. Grammar in the Learning of Correct Usage." **Journal of Eduational Psychology**, 22 (1931), 81-96.

Thomsom, Jack. "Social Class Labelling in the Application of Bernstein's Theory of Codes to the Identification of Linguistic Advantage and Disadvantage in Five Year Old Children." **Educational Research**, 29, 4 (November 1977), 273-83.

Tobin, James. "Reaganomics and Economics." **New York Review of Books**, 28, 19 (December 3, 1981), 11-5.

Trilling, Lionel. "The Two Environments: Reflections on the Study of English." **Encounter**, 25, 1 (July 1965), 3-13.

Troike, Rudolph C. "Receptive Competence, Productive Competence, and Performance." In James Alatis (ed.), **Report of the Twentieth Annual Round Table Meeting On Linguistics and Language Study**. Washington: Georgetown University Press, 1970.

Vernon, M. "Fifty Years of Research On the Intelligence of Deaf and Hard of Hearing Children: A Review of the Literature and Discussion of Implications." **Journal of Rehabilitation of the Deaf**, 1 (1968), 1-12.

Vygotsky, Lev S. **Thought and Language**. Ed. and trans. E. Hanfmann and G. Vakar. Cambridge, Mass.: MIT Press, 1962.

Walker, L., Paddock, H., Brown, L. and Baksh, I. "Nonstandard Dialect and Literacy; An Inservice Project in Newfoundland." **Interchange**, 6, 3 (1975), 4-10.

Watt, Ian. "The Reading Public and the Rise of the Novel." In Elizabeth and Tom Burns (eds.), **Sociology of Literature and Drama**. Hammondsworth: Penguin, 1973, pp. 402-17.

Weener, P. **The Influence of Dialect Differences On the Immediate Recall of Verbal Messages**. Unpublished doctoral dissertation. University of Michigan, 1967.

Whorf, Benjamin Lee. **Language, Thought and Reality: Selected Writings**. Ed. John Carroll. Cambridge Mass.: MIT Press, 1956.

Wilkinson, Andrew. **The Foundations of Language: Talking and Reading in Young Children**. Oxford: Oxford University Press, 1972.

Williams, Frederick. "The Identification of Linguistic Attitudes." **Linguistics**, 136 (September 1974), 21-32.

Willinsky, John M. "Authority and Ideology as a Source of Certainty: A Response to James Heap." **Curriculum Inquiry**, 11, 3 (1981), 223-26.

Willis, Paul. **Learning to Labour**. Farnborough, England: Saxon House, 1977.

Wittgenstein, Ludwig. **Philosophical Investigations**. 3rd ed. Trans. G. E. M. Anscombe. New York: Macmillan, 1958.

Index